My Enemy—My Self

Overcoming Your Self-Defeating Mind

The Psychology of Self-Change

C. Franklin Truan, PhD

My Enemy, My Self: Overcoming Your Self-Defeating Mind; The Psychology of Self-Change

Published by Wheatmark®
1760 East River Road, Suite 145, Tucson, Arizona 85718 U.S.A.
www.wheatmark.com

ISBN: 978-1-62787-048-1 (paperback)
ISBN: 978-1-62787-064-1 (ebook)
LCCN: 2013918565

To my wife, Sheila, for inspiring me to share my ideas for making people's lives more fulfilling; for her insight and helpful perspective, which challenged me to better communicate my ideas to my readers; for her tireless editing; for her ability to be a happy person; and for helping to make our life together a fulfilling experience.

Contents

Preface ix

Introduction. 1
  Psychological Quality: An Individual Choice. 1
  Make Your Choice—the Quality of Your Life Depends on It 5
  Courage: A Choice 6

1   The Nature and Development of Your Self 9
    Your Self Is in Your Mind. 9
    The Three Facets of One's Self. 12
    A Pictorial Look at the Self. 13
    Definition of Terms about the Self 14
    Self-Esteem 15
    Self-Efficacy. 16
    Self-Advocacy. 17
    Self-Respect. 17
    Self-Confidence 18
    The Development of a Healthy Self. 18
    The Power of Belief. 21
    The Development of a Troubled Self. 23
    Developmental Consequences of a Troubled Primitive-Self. 26
    Signs and Symptoms of a Troubled Self 28

2   Elements of a Divided, Troubled Self: The Self in
    Conflict 30
    A Divided, Troubled Self 30
    Origin of a Troubled Self 34
    More Signs of a Troubled Self 36
    Fear as a Primary Motivator 38
    Connecting with your Primitive-Self 39
    The Troubled Surface-Self 43
    Primitive-Self and Resistance to Real Change 44
    In Summary. 46

3   Your Mind: Ally or Enemy?. 48
    The Basic Functions of the Mind. 48
    Thinking, Feeling, and Acting—a Microcosm of Life. 49
    Thinking versus Feeling?. 50
    Feelings—a Dubious Source for Truth. 52
    Unreasoned Thinking 53
    Valuing Reasoning 56
    A Primer on Truth 57
    Identifying Truth through Reasoned Thinking 61
    In Summary. 65

4   The Meta-Self 67
    Sound Thinking and Faulty Thinking. 67
    Trust and Self-Efficacy 68
    The Meta-Self. 69
    Meta-Self Characteristics 73
    Developing Conscious Principles in your Meta-Self. 79
    Universal Meta-Principles. 80
    Living Meta-Self Principles and Values. 80
    Meta-Self Skills: Empathy. 81
    The Meta-Self in Relationships 83
    In Summary. 83

5   The Process of Changing Your Self 85
    Make a Commitment to Real Change 85
    Seek and Live Truth. 87
    Learning to Identify the Facets of One's Self 89
    Time Out. 92
    Connecting with Your Real Self. 93

Contents

Monitoring Your Feeling Experiences............................94
Building a Feeling-Word Vocabulary..........................95
Journaling to You about You..................................97
Example 1: Ted's Journal Entry, (Week 2).....................99
Example 2: Sara's Journal Entry, (Week 3)...................100
Identifying Core Beliefs.....................................101
Identifying Core Beliefs of Your Primitive-Self..............103
Reading..103
Writing..104
Behavior Observation.......................................104
Observing and Responding to Feelings and Reasons Observed
in Others...105
In Summary...106

6 **Conscious Development of Your Meta-Self.............109**
What You Have Learned So Far..............................109
The Meta-Self: Establishing Healthy Beliefs as Principles for
Living..112
Building Your Meta-Self....................................113
Reasoning versus Childhood and Cultural Beliefs..............114
Universal Meta-Self Principles..............................116
Other Suggested Meta-Self Principles—A Starter List.........117
Constructing Meta-Self Principles..........................119
Your Meta-Self's Role as Parent to Your Primitive-Self.........120
Cognitive Exercise for Your Meta-Self.......................121
Learning from Regressive Episodes..........................122
Building Your Meta-Self Through Interpersonal Skills
Development..125
Objective Listening Skills...................................126
Discrimination Skills.......................................127
Empathetic Communication Skills...........................127
Building your Meta-Self—Program Development Skills........128
In Summary...129

Afterword 133
In Closing..136
Universal Meta-Self Principles..............................136
Major Meta-Self Principles..................................137

Contents

Appendix A: Sample of Feeling Words 139

Appendix B: Suggested Reading 142
Reading to Promote Connection with Real Self 142
Reading about Reasoned Thinking and Logic 142
Additional Reading in Psychology 142
Program Development Skills 142

About the Author 143

Preface

We did not choose life; neither were we born knowing how to live it. To be alive is a gift that each of us experiences in our own unique way. It is up to each of us to make sense of our experience and to use the gift of life in nourishing, beneficial ways.

To find fulfillment in life we must learn to use our minds effectively to make constructive sense of the world and our own experience of ourselves. Most importantly, one's mind must be able to discern functional truth. The ability to identify what is really true makes it possible for us to have faith in our mind's abilities and, therefore, trust in ourselves. Once you have trust in yourself, you have the ability to trust others. *Thus, it is the quality of our thinking that determines the quality of our experience of life.*

For better or worse, our ability to think and the content of our core beliefs are both learned early in life. The quality of our thinking ability and content is profoundly influenced and shaped by the nurturing abilities of our primary caregivers. We build upon this foundation as we proceed through our lives.

If your family-of-origin nurturing was appropriate and loving, you learned to value and trust yourself. Valuing yourself forms the necessary psychological foundation for healthy growth and development throughout life. Having faith in yourself and in your mind's ability to guide you makes it possible to successfully meet the challenges that life presents. Given the opportunity, in the form of a psychologically nourishing early environment, an individual will develop a positive sense of who he is and a functional set of knowledge and skills for interacting effectively with the outside world. He will also learn to psychologically nourish others and be nourished in return. He will experience a full and rewarding life—he will experience a life of *psychological quality*.

In reality, too many people do not experience lives of psychological quality. What they learned to believe about themselves in early childhood was not positive and beneficial. It was negative and harmful. As a direct result, the quality of their psychological development and experience of life has been negatively affected by these early learned beliefs. If your initial nurturing was lacking, then you learned, to some degree, to devalue yourself and your abilities. As a consequence, you approach life's challenges in self-defeating and perhaps even self-destructive ways. If you experience, for instance, recurring issues with your loved ones, subordinates, peers, or superiors, these problems are symptomatic of deficiencies in the quality of your thinking processes or in the negative nature of your thinking.

People with thinking deficiencies and negative beliefs about themselves want to experience psychological quality, but their faulty thinking makes it impossible. Their own minds work against achieving what they need and desire most. They become their own enemies. Consequently, their lives are filled with discouragement, failure, disillusionment, and in many cases, self-destructive thinking and behaviors.

It would be easy for you to say at this point that you, of course, like and value yourself. I am sure you would also say that you do your best to solve problems and improve your life. Are you being truthful with yourself? There is something about you that made you want to read this book—maybe something that you want to change but don't know how. Or maybe there is something that you have repeatedly tried to solve on your own and found it impossible. Perhaps you have been looking for solutions in the wrong places. Perhaps you are attempting to solve the wrong problems. Perhaps the problems and the solutions are really within you—and about you.

What you believe to be the truth about you—the value you place on you as an individual—controls your destiny and the quality of your existence throughout life. The good news is that you can change yourself and your life for the better. Regardless of what happened to you in the past, it is within your power to correct the damage. It is your choice and responsibility to shape the quality of your present and future. This book has been written for people who need and, most importantly, want help in making their lives healthier, happier, and a more fulfilling experience—those who want to experience psychological quality.

Introduction

For better or worse, early learned beliefs
define what you believe to be true about you, the person.
Once established, these beliefs control your destiny.

Psychological Quality: An Individual Choice

As human beings we all share two fundamental but profound psychological life goals. We all want to value who we are as people, and we want to experience nourishment and fulfillment through relating well with others. People who live with poor perceptions of themselves—negative self-concepts—are unable to achieve these goals.

Improving one's self-concept is a difficult challenge. It is difficult because it requires both the *desire* and the *ability* to change who you are, how you see yourself as a person. It requires an openness to seeing and owning the real you, and openness to new knowledge that will challenge what you currently accept as truth. It requires the courage to face the unknown.

Real, beneficial, and enduring self-change begins with acceptance of the psychological "three R's" as new life values. No, not "Reading, 'Riting, and 'Rithmetic." Rather, I'm referring to the Three R's for psychological health and fulfillment—Responsibility, Reasoning, and Reality. First, you must accept *responsibility* for the direction and quality of your present and future life. You must also learn to value and practice *reasoned* thinking as the only way to identify truth and direct your life. Finally, you must learn to identify and conform to what is *real and true* instead of believing what you want to.

Consider the following questions:

» Do you feel good about who you really are?

» Do you feel like you are one person inside?

» Are you able to resolve inner conflicts without the help of others?

» Do you trust your mind to make sound decisions?

» Are you able to foster and maintain fulfilling relationships?

» Do you do what is right for you even if it displeases others?

» Is your life on a good psychological path for the future?

» Do you display your real self to others?

» Does the emotional age you feel match your chronological age?

» Are you a person worth loving?

» Do you believe you are valuable—as a person?

If you answered no to one or more of these questions, it is an indicator of a troubled, divided self—a self that is, at a minimum, underdeveloped, and probably psychologically and interpersonally impaired. If you can accept that at least part of the problem is within you, you have achieved the first step in really changing the quality of your life. Accepting responsibility for being the cause of your problems means you are open to seeing the real you. You are ready to begin identifying and owning what you value and do not value about you. You are ready to know and evaluate the quality of your beliefs about you and the world. You are ready to begin the journey toward increasing the quality of your experience of you, your experience with others, and your experience of life in general.

Improving the quality of your psychological life for the better is a difficult challenge because it demands changing much of what you now believe to be true about yourself. Who you learned to be—what you learned in early life as truth about you and what was therefore possible for you in the world—is ingrained in the deepest levels of your mind. Those early learned beliefs are hardwired in your being—your definition of existence. Once established, they control your destiny—even if they are destructive to you.

Early learned beliefs form your perceptions of reality, and once in place, everything you observe is filtered through their perceptual window. Your early learned beliefs influence every decision you make in life. To be beneficial, these beliefs must not deny *actual* reality, be harmful to you, or limit your psychological development as a human being. Healthful early learned beliefs enable you to make rational and constructive sense of your experience of yourself and the outside world. They give you direction toward achieving all that life has to offer. They allow you to develop psychologically toward becoming a mentally sound and mature adult.

When your beliefs about yourself or the world are negative, normal psychological development is impaired . Your ability to feel good about yourself and meet the challenges presented by life diminishes with each passing year. Failures mount, and discouragement grows. Solution after solution may be attempted to change your life for the better, but nothing really works. Over time, your actions become increasingly harmful to you and others. Your thoughts and feelings become more negative and confused, yet you deny or avoid the real truth about you. Eventually all your attempts to deny or escape your troubles will fail.

Having a negative self-concept is not a rare phenomenon. It limits, damages or destroys the lives of millions. Negative self-concepts take on a variety of forms and are evident and abundant in all societies. In fact, more than half of all people hold predominately negative beliefs about themselves. Too often, the solution to a negative self-concept is to deny its existence and to find an escape in a destructive behavior that only complicates the problem. To escape from troubled thoughts and behavior, people use alcohol, medications, emotional and physical isolation, overeating, overworking, or other addictive and destructive behaviors. The prevalence of drugs, both legal and illegal, and even the failure of the national "war on drugs," are persuasive evidence of the many millions who are unhappy with their lives. Their underlying goal for their destructive behaviors is always the same—*to escape from their real selves.*

Such mistaken solutions only make life increasingly worse for the individual and for all those who relate with him. If these self-defeating thoughts and behaviors progress too far, they cannot be reversed. The individual is destined for self-destruction.

Many other troubled individuals, who are not as obvious as those with addictions, are people who are constantly negative about themselves or others. Being chronically negative about yourself or others is a destructive lifestyle based on conscious or subconscious irrational beliefs. What are the irrational beliefs held by critical people? Everyone has their own, but here are a couple of common examples: At a subconscious level, one might believe, "Being negative and critical about others proves to me and others that I am a better person." Or, at a conscious level, "I'm just a person who tells the truth, and people don't like it."

In truth, thinking or talking negatively to an excessive extent about others is a learned way of attempting to feel better about you. However, being excessively critical does not really make anyone feel better about who they are. If it did, they would not have to continue the behavior. In reality, it only provides surface relief as a temporary distraction or escape from the reality of a troubled self. With time, being critical alienates the negative person from others. Given enough time, the individual will also become *consciously* disgusted with himself. You cannot escape forever from your real self—what you believe to be the truth about you. Neither can you escape the eventual consequences of your negative, harmful behavior. You can blame, and you can deny, but you cannot hide forever from the truth.

Last, but not least, is the effect of a negative self-concept on building trust in one's mind to know truth. A negative mind denies the value of truth and reasoning. It accepts only what agrees with it in the moment—with its current reality. An individual who thinks negatively does not see his contradictory thinking or his flexibility with what is true at any given moment. Because a negative mind constructs conflicting truths or avoids truth to suit its immediate needs, it can never know real truth. Consequently, an irrational, negative mind cannot trust its own thinking processes. At the subconscious core, a person with a mind that cannot be trusted to know truth lives in fear—the fear of not knowing. *Fear, conscious and subconscious, becomes the primary motivator for all thinking, feeling, and action.*

By the way, do you know what the opposite of fear is? If you have trouble coming up with the answer to this question, there is a good probability that fear is *your* primary motivator in life. At the worst levels of dysfunction, people motivated by fear are not consciously aware of their fear. Fear resides deep in their minds at a subconscious level, and most of their mental energy is spent avoiding anything that would put them in touch with the conscious experience of it. At a lesser degree of impairment, where individuals are aware of being afraid, considerable energy is spent avoiding situations and subjects that could invoke fear. Fear as a primary motivator is a debilitating and destructive force over the course of life. Its existence is a significant sign of a divided, troubled self.

Do you relate with the experience of these unhappy people? Are you able to own your own unhappiness? Does fear dominate your life? Do you want to do something about it? If you are not happy with yourself or your inability to relate effectively with others, it is your choice and your responsibility to change the course of your life. Remember, it doesn't matter how you got to this point in your life or who in your past may have contributed to your current condition. You cannot change the quality of your life by wallowing in your misery or blaming others. It is up to you to take responsibility and change yourself and your life for the better.

Make Your Choice—the Quality of Your Life Depends on It

Ask yourself, as though your life were almost over and you were assessing the quality of your time on earth, "What really made my life worthwhile? Where did I find quality?" What will your answer be? I believe the only answer that captures the most fundamental truth—the one that reflects whether the experience of life was one of quality—can be found in the degree of quality you experienced *with yourself and with a few significant others.* The amount of money you accumulated or how many material goods you possess become meaningless when compared to how you feel about you and how you feel about your ability to give to those few people you have really cared about.

Fundamental to the experience of a life of psychological quality is *feeling good about who you are*. To have a positive self-concept is to have faith in *who you are as a person* and to genuinely value yourself. A positive sense of self—a positive self-concept—is the most important psychological element in fostering mental health and maintaining it. Mental illnesses and chronic interpersonal problems of all types can be traced to an underlying poor self-concept.

A positive, secure sense of self is also fundamental to the experience of genuine emotional intimacy with another human being. With a negative sense of self, an individual is so preoccupied with himself that empathy, the most necessary ability for experiencing real intimacy with others, is not possible. Without empathy, relationships remain superficial and are viewed as self-serving places to get what one needs or wants without regard for the other person. People with negative self-concepts are *takers* in relationships—not givers. Their focus in relationships is on how to manipulate and control to get what they want. (This is true even if they see themselves as helpless.) In the process of relating, they refuse to take any real responsibility for their own deficits and are experts at blaming others and putting them on the defensive. However, at the deeper levels of their real selves, they see themselves as undeserving or unlovable. They believe they are harmful or destructive to others, and their harmful surface behavior confirms their belief.

Courage: A Choice

The opposite of fear is *courage*. Psychologically healthy people (and those who want to be) are motivated by courage—the courage to know the truth about their real selves and challenge anything they discover that impedes their health and fulfillment as human beings. To them, fears are to be identified, challenged, and overcome. They have courage as a primary motivator because they have faith in themselves and faith in their ability to relate well with others. They have courage because they trust their own minds to know truth and guide them accordingly. They display the courage to attempt anything that will make their lives richer and more rewarding. They consistently challenge adversity and grow as human beings from the experience. They experience lives of valuing and respecting themselves. Psychologically healthy people are adept at fulfilling their own needs and desires while respecting the rights and needs of others. They have the ability to live a life of psychological quality.

Experiencing psychological quality, changing yourself for the better, means changing the way you think about yourself and the world. It means altering your faulty beliefs that make you feel bad about who you are and limit your ability to be psychologically sound and to grow to psychological maturity. Changing your core beliefs will change everything else in your life, and only you have the power to do it. Because you are chronologically an adult, no one else can make you change who you are. Only you have the power to take responsibility for making your life better and feeling good about being you. You are the one who must make the decision to be healthy, to have courage, to work toward a life of psychological quality. By the way, if you do nothing to make your life better, you are also responsible for that.

The first step in this process of self-change is to admit that you are less than who you want to be. You must take responsibility for who you are and who you are not. Only your honest opinion, the truth about you, matters. You must first own what is true about you. Ask yourself, "What is good about me *as a person* that I value and want to keep? What do I not like about me that I want to change?"

It is my experience that as many as half of all people, regardless of class or culture, are dissatisfied with the way their lives have evolved and the state of discontentment in which they exist. It is also my experience that at the core of the perceived problems, these people are all too often unhappy about who they are *as people*. They have never really liked who they are, and they fear who they are becoming. They are sad, discouraged, or defeated by

7

their experience of life and their experience of themselves. Their crisis is chronic and acute—long-term and immediate.

More often than not, the real problems and the real solutions for these troubled people can be found in their own minds. If you have a mind that does not value you and works against your finding fulfillment in life, it is not your ally. If your mind works against you, it is not your friend—it is your enemy. All in life that is good begins with you believing in your own value.

If you are unhappy, depressed, or clinically impaired, at least part, if not all, of the problem rests in faulty beliefs held as truth in your mind. Through no fault of your own, and very early in life, you may have learned false, irrational, and destructive beliefs about yourself and the world in general. You have remained trapped by these negative, self-destructive beliefs that you accepted as reality as a child and still use to govern the course of your life.

This book is an exploration of the major problematic outcomes generated by poor or negative self-concept, and it presents the common-sense solution to the problems that plague individuals with a negative sense of self. The solution to a self-limiting and eventually self-destructive life script begins with taking responsibility for knowing the real you—the true nature of your own mind. You must assess the validity and functionality of your hidden beliefs that guide your every thought, feeling, and action.

Finally, you must construct a rational, healthy, adult self, a *Meta-Self*, that is built on functional reality and reasoned thinking. Once there is a healthier sense of self in place, you can begin to experience joy and fulfillment that grows out of a positive, rational, and reality-based belief structure. You will begin to feel good about being you.

1

The Nature and Development of Your Self

The "self" is the collection of core subjective beliefs that an individual holds as truth about his or her self.

Those who have been fortunate enough to develop and experience psychological quality as a constant in their lives know the importance of valuing one's self. They understand that valuing one's self is the prerequisite for being able to love others and believing they are worthy of being loved. Because they believe in their value as a person, they have been able to learn to trust the ability of their own minds to know truth. They do not accept what others have taught them in the past without regard for its validity and consequences. They accept only truth that is based on the acceptance of reality and their own reasoned thinking. Finally, they own that it is their individual responsibility to shape their present and future experiences for the better. They have become their own allies and advocates.

Your Self Is in Your Mind

The challenge of understanding and changing your life for the better must begin with some essential information concerning the nature and workings of your mind—the location of your self.

The human brain is the physical object in which the mind resides. On the other hand, the human mind is the mental content of the brain—the thoughts and feelings it creates. One's mind is in constant motion perceiving, ordering, and choosing among all the information it takes in so it can perform specific tasks. The mind's content is a collection of subjectively perceived and processed information that develops in the form of beliefs that provide understanding and meaning for its owner.

One's mind makes sense out of the individual's experience of himself and the world around him. The products of this process are the beliefs the individual holds as truth. A person's earliest learned beliefs about himself and the world are the most important ones. They are the core beliefs from which all others are developed. Their quality, the positive or negative valence and degree of rationality, determines the course of psychological development over one's lifetime.

In learning about the content of the mind, the process of perceiving, ordering, and making sense out of observed facts is a subjective—not objective—thinking process. I am certain that you would agree that people do not perceive or interpret actions or events in the same way. They draw different conclusions and meanings from the same incident. Each person's biased thinking and uniqueness influences how they perceive, interpret, and attribute meaning to anything. Individual experiences, attitudes, temperaments, intelligence (intellectual and psychological), and environmental influences cause variance in what people perceive. Obviously then, because we all process and arrive at perceived truth individually, the quality of one's subjective thinking is again so important.

As soon as life begins, an individual's mind begins the subjective process of creating the self. The meaning of the term "self" is not an easy concept to understand. In the most general sense, the self is the collection of core subjective beliefs that an individual holds as truth about himself. The content of these core beliefs defines one's self-concept; that is, what you believe to be true about yourself. By default, a person's self-concept will be either primarily positive or negative. Self-concept is the total sum of an individual's subjective perception of himself or herself; that is, his or her perceived value as a human being and his or her perceived capabilities. Self-concept personally defines reality for each individual. It determines "who I really am and what I see as appropriate and possible for me in life." Simply stated, you are what you believe, and you can only become what you believe is possible for you.

In human beings, one's self-concept filters all experiences of life:

» If an individual's self-concept is positive, experiences of all types will be internally processed beneficially, and the course of psychological development as a person will happen normally in a healthful manner and direction.

» If an individual's self-concept is negative, all experience is filtered through a negative perception of self. This leads to a variety of problematic outcomes.

We must distinguish the concept of self from the more familiar terms of personality or character. Personality or character is the set of characteristics (behaviors) of a person that makes him unique. These broader concepts describe how others see a person as well as how he envisions himself. The perception of self is more personal and private, because only the individual knows its real nature. Finally, the characteristics and competencies an individual believes as truth about his self dominates all outside perceptions.

The self's continuing function makes sense of observed reality and masters the tasks presented by reality through organizing and reorganizing experience. The individual must make sense out of both the outside world and his continually developing inner sense of self, which is both a cognitive and emotional learning process. The individual's actual and perceived degree of quality of self will affect his ability to perform these mental tasks in a healthful way. If an individual has a positive self-concept based on an accurate awareness of reality, then normal psychological development can occur. The person will grow to value himself and trust in the ability of his mind to know truth, and it will guide him through a fulfilling life. If an individual develops a negative self-concept early in life, all future experiences will be adversely affected.

The Three Facets of One's Self

An individual's mental self, the content of his mind, can be divided into three elements or facets:

» The *Primitive-Self*, or child self, is the facet of your mind that develops first. The Primitive-Self becomes the foundation upon which the other facets of one's self are built. The quality of the Primitive-Self, its level of mental soundness, affects the development and quality of the other facets of one's self—the Surface-Self and Meta-Self.

» The *Surface-Self* is the portion of one's mind that is presented to and interacts with the outside world. In early childhood, before the age of six, it is an open reflection of the Primitive-Self. Around the age of six, a child gains an awareness of his self for the first time. If his self-awareness is troubled (negative), the Surface-Self will develop as an agent in collusion with a troubled Primitive-Self. Its primary focus will be to hide the troubled self. If the child has a positive sense of self, his psychological development will proceed in a healthy direction: the Surface-Self will accurately represent the healthy Primitive-Self. As the child grows to adulthood, a healthy Meta-Self will be formed, and the Surface-Self will become the agent of the healthy Meta-Self. It will effectively perform its function to interact in healthful ways with the outside world.

» The *Meta-Self* is the rational, healthy, competent, responsible, and eventually mature facet of one's mind. The Meta-Self's development begins as a part of a healthy Primitive-Self, but as one matures psychologically, it takes over as governor of all thinking, feeling, and behavioral processes. As healthy psychological development occurs by chronological adulthood, the Meta-Self is well seated as the dominant facet of one's mind.

A Pictorial Look at the Self

The following are pictorial illustrations (Venn diagrams) of the psychologically healthy self and troubled self. Venn diagrams use circles to represent the logical relationship between elements of a whole. In this case, the Venn diagrams present the relationship of the elements or facets of the self. The Primitive, Surface, and Meta selves are the mind's content elements that comprise the whole self.

The first diagram is that of a healthy self with the Meta-Self as the largest and most powerful portion of the whole self. The Primitive-Self is present as a part of the individual's self, but its small size relative to the Meta-Self represents its lack of power to control and direct the psychologically healthy and mature mind.

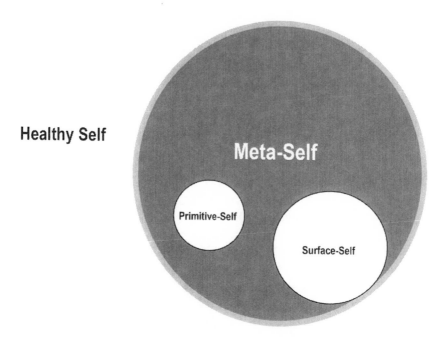

Healthy Self

In the second diagram (troubled self), the Primitive-Self is the most dominant portion of the self. It holds immature, irrational, and destructive power over all thinking, feeling, and behavior. In such a mind, the Meta-Self has never developed or remains undeveloped and without sufficient power to influence or direct the individual's thoughts, feelings, and behavior in healthful ways.

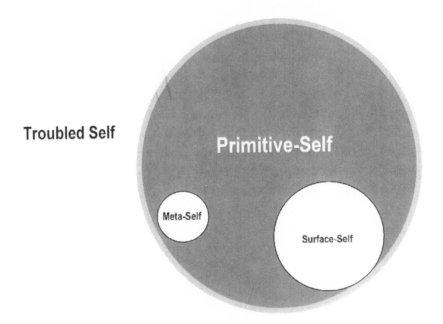

Whether psychologically healthy or troubled, the above descriptions and diagrams form a context and foundation for understanding the relationship among the facets of one's self.

Definition of Terms about the Self

There are several other terms used to describe various aspects of self. They are content elements of the individual's belief system. Together they compose one's total self-concept. These content elements include *self-esteem, self-efficacy, self-advocacy, self-respect, and self-confidence.* These elements of a person's self are also subjectively formed and are all interconnected and interdependent.

Self-Esteem

Self-esteem is the *subjectively perceived* value a person attributes to himself, as a person. An individual's potential to develop and sustain psychological quality is fundamentally related to his perception of his level of self-esteem. Self-esteem is the degree of value or worth you perceive in yourself as a human being. For example, do you genuinely like and love yourself as a person? Do you see yourself as worthy of being loved? Do you say you like something about yourself but secretly don't trust it or secretly know it contradicts something else you believe?

High self-esteem is expressed in the following ways:

» In your facial expressions, physical appearance, and manner, and a way of talking and moving that projects the pleasure one takes in being alive

» In ease in talking about your own accomplishments and shortcomings with directness and honesty

» In the comfort and ease you experience in giving and receiving compliments, expressions of affection, and appreciation

» In your openness to criticism and an ability to admit mistakes

» In your words and movements having a quality of ease and spontaneity, reflecting that you are not at war with yourself

» In the congruence (harmony) between what you say and do, and how you look, sound, and move

» In an attitude of openness to and curiosity about new ideas, new experiences, and new possibilities in life

» In the fact that feelings of anxiety or insecurity will be less likely to intimidate or overwhelm, that negative feelings are just information to be understood, evaluated, and managed

» In an ability to enjoy the humorous aspects of life, in one's self as well as those seen in others

» In the ability to be flexible in responding to problems and challenges

» In your comfort with assertive behavior in yourself as well as in others

» In your ability to preserve a quality of self composure, objectivity, and empathy for yourself and others while under conditions of stress

» In your belief that you are as valuable a person as anyone else

Self-Efficacy

Self-efficacy is the amount of trust or faith a person has in his own mental thought processes, as well as the trust he has in the validity of his mind's conclusions. Am I able to make objective, accurate judgments about myself and the world? Do I trust the validity of my beliefs, my decisions, and the actions based upon them? A mentally healthy person's cognitive abilities include the ability to think objectively and rationally while constructively integrating subjective thoughts and feelings. He makes decisions with clarity and confidence. He is confident that his thinking will lead to constructive and beneficial actions. This individual has faith in the thought processes and conclusions of his mind.

Clear and confident thinking also enables confident communication with others in a concrete and logical manner. The individual with high self-efficacy experiences thought processes that are confirmed by consistent competence and success in the outside world, and by the inner experience of feeling good about who he is.

High self-efficacy is expressed in the following ways:

» In your demonstrated ability to trust your mind to know beneficial, practical truth in any situation

» In your ability and choice to use your own reasoned thinking to make decisions and judgments

» In your ability to trust your mind to function adequately, even when you are highly stressed or emotional

» In your ability to decide and know what is best for you and to have faith in your knowing

» In your belief in your ability to learn anything you need or want to know

Self-Advocacy

Self-advocacy is being your own best ally. Self-advocacy is believing in the value of yourself and your responsibility to hold yourself accountable for acting on that belief. When you are your own advocate, you have your best interest at heart and you will not defeat your attempts to succeed or grow as a person. You guide yourself productively through new experience and understanding. You are constructively self-critical enough to identify deficits, but you are also accepting of your present self while you pursue growth. You hold yourself accountable for doing what is right and what is healthful for you and others. You maintain a positive personal sense of responsibility over the nature and quality of your thinking, feeling, and actions. You are committed to having a valid positive perception of yourself. *Self-advocacy is a critical element in building a positive self-concept, especially for those who start from a long history of negative thinking about themselves.*

Self-Respect

Self-respect concerns the value you demonstrate about you, the person. With a high degree of self-respect you project the good thoughts and feelings you have about you. You also expect and require others to treat you with respect, kindness, and fairness. If necessary, you *demand* respect from those who do not give it to you.

Self-Confidence

In general, self-confidence is the pride and assurance you feel and project about you, the person. At a surface level self-confidence is the assurance of high-level competence you have, based on proven ability in a specific area. Intellectual tasks, specific-area expertise, and individual talents are examples of where an individual's self-confidence is evident. *Be advised, having Surface-Self-confidence about your competence in a specific area does not ensure or even imply having a good overall self-concept.*

The Development of a Healthy Self

*I have value as a person, and therefore I am
worthy of being loved.*

Before introducing in detail the topic of the troubled self and how to change it for the better, it is important to understand some basics about the normal, healthy process of psychological self-development.

Development of one's self happens in stages. The first stage of self-development is the forming of the Primitive-Self. Emergence of the Primitive-Self begins most likely when a child is in a fetal state. A child in the womb of its mother is subject to many developmental factors that may contribute to self-development. The most important element may be the mother's psychological health and the effect of her emotional state on the developing fetus. However, at the present time there is little scientific evidence to confirm this possibility.

Developmental factors that are supported by science and common sense are both genetically inherited and physical. The mother's health, nutrition, and habits are the most obvious physical factors. Inherited traits include potential for intelligence (both psychological and intellectual), temperament (passive to aggressive behavioral tendencies), physical abilities, and special talents.

As stated above, less is known for certain about the influence of the mother's emotional or psychological self on the developing fetus. However, from the moment of birth, the mother's mental health and the quality of her every interaction with the infant has an effect for better or worse on the formation of self. This interaction effect is true of all primary caregivers immediately and continuously involved with the infant or young child. The nature and quality of one's Primitive-Self is a product of interactions with significant others experienced during the first few years of life.

To sum up, one's primitive sense of self consists of a blending of inherited traits or characteristics determined before birth and the type and quality of interactions experienced during the early years of life. Inherited traits can be enhanced or limited by the quality of primary social interactions; therefore, the quality of parenting (primary caregiving) is crucial in the development of a healthy sense of self. Parents or other caregivers who are themselves psychologically healthy and interpersonally competent are much more likely to rear emotionally healthy children. Primary caregivers who are psychologically impaired are bound to have a negative influence on a developing child. For example, how can you teach a child to have good self-esteem if you do not have it yourself?

The Primitive-Self in the first few years of life is best described as a work in progress. During the first eighteen months of life, the infant's perception of self as a separate person has not yet happened. A child sees himself as an extension of the people that care for him. Thus you can see that from the beginning, the mental health and behaviors displayed by significant others around the infant have a great effect on the formation of self. The mental health of the primary caregivers, and the quality of psychological care given, combine with inherited traits acquired by chance from the biological parents to form the Primitive-Self.

When a child's early psychological environment is as it should be, psychological development of the Primitive-Self proceeds according to natural human characteristics. Through gradual experiencing, the evolving self constructively shapes itself and its perception of the world. The individual proceeds normally to develop a Primitive-Self that has a positive set of beliefs about himself and a basic, functional working knowledge of internal and external reality. Consequently, during the various stages of psychological development the child is able to successfully meet life's challenges. He feels good about who he is, knows right from wrong, and learns to trust his mind to know how to solve the challenges that life presents. In contrast, a psychologically troubled Primitive-Self, in any form and degree, is evidence of the failure of this natural development and resulting competence to occur.

A child reared in a mentally healthy and nourishing home, where effective parental figures are appropriately responsive, will develop a Primitive-Self that includes a positive, secure sense of self. For example, effective parents know the importance of separating the child, as a person, from the child's behavior. They understand that valuing their child, as a person, is demonstrated by the communication of unconditional love for the person in spite of his behavior. They know that the child's feelings are simply information about his emotional state and that his behavior is only an expression of his thoughts and feelings. They are separate from his quality as a person. He is not a bad person just because he is angry or misbehaves. He is not a good person just because he is doing what his parents want him to do. Effective parents consistently communicate the child's value as a person while they respond appropriately to shape both his self-concept and his behavior. In a healthy home a child experiences being valued as a person and learns how to perceive, manage, and express himself positively and appropriately. Because the child can trust his parents' valuing of him, he will also develop trust in himself and his own growing mental abilities.

Because of yet undeveloped cognitive ability and the dominance of the Primitive-Self, a child in the first few years of life is driven primarily by immediate feelings. As the child develops cognitively, his thoughts and behavior become more and more ordered and complex. If the primary caregivers are able to respond appropriately to successive stages of his emotional and cognitive development, then he continues to build upon a positive set of beliefs about himself and his abilities. With the consistent experience of feeling valued, the child will in time believe in his *right to be valued*, because he believes in his own value. The belief of having and deserving value is a fundamental, critical building block of a positive self-concept. A child's positive sense of self lays the groundwork for all future beneficial psychological development. The experience of feeling valued is the beginning of believing one's self to be loved and therefore loveable.

The child's acquired belief is that "I have value as a person, and therefore I am worthy of being loved." Having one's thoughts and feelings about one's self positively validated sets the stage for trusting one's mind to function effectively (self-efficacy). So, being valued and feeling valuable spark faith in one's mind and in one's self.

The Power of Belief

The individual's early-acquired Primitive-Self-concept defines reality—the truth about who he is and who he can be. This set of personal beliefs is composed of many thoughts and feelings, organized into general beliefs about himself and the world. They define not only his perceived value as a person but also his perceived potential for all that life offers. An individual's beliefs concerning his self can be positive, productive, and beneficial to him and others, or they can be negative, limiting, and destructive. Following are questions that are *consciously or subconsciously* answered, for better or worse, by every individual at a young age and repeatedly throughout life.

Questions every individual continuously asks and must answer:

- » Am I a bad or a good person?

- » Am I deserving of love?

- » Am I able to love others?

- » Do I have a sound mind?

- » How intelligent am I?

- » In what areas am I gifted or talented?

- » In what areas am I not so bright?

- » Am I an emotionally strong person?

» Do my emotional and actual ages match?

» Do others like me?

» Am I motivated by fear or courage?

» What do I fear?

» Am I a risk-taker?

» How attractive am I?

» Do I relate well with others?

» Can I make good decisions without help from others?

» Am I competent in one or more areas of potential achievement?

» Can I trust my thinking processes?

» What is my attitude about life in general?

It is these beliefs—the subjective content of one's mind—that determine the quality of existence, achievement, and fulfillment we consider possible for ourselves. Once answered and accepted as truth, these beliefs form the individual's self-identity, for better or worse. Subsequent thinking and resulting behavior reinforce and confirm one's perceived identity. When the Primitive-Self gets a healthy beginning, the stage is set for healthy development of the individual's Surface-Self and Meta-Self. A positive Primitive-Self—being in touch with one's real self, feeling safe, feeling valued, and trusting in one's mind—forms the necessary foundation for the creation and constructive growth of a Meta-Self. If all goes well, by the time a child reaches adulthood, the Meta-Self will be well under way to assuming constructive control of all thinking and behaving.

The Development of a Troubled Self

*A child chooses separation from the real self
out of the necessity for survival, and this is the
beginning of a divided, conflicted, negative
self.*

Most psychological disorders, emotional problems, and inter-personal deficits originate in one's experience within the family of origin. Fundamental psychological pathologies and emotional deficits are passed on interpersonally from generation to generation. Poor parenting, in the form of psychological pathology or ignorance, is the most prevalent cause of mental illness and emotional and interpersonal deficits; this means that they are primarily acquired or learned and not genetically inherited. The predominant observable symptom of having received less than adequate parenting is having a negative self-concept. Poor or dysfunctional psychological caregiving in early life always results, in some degree, to the formation of a negative self-concept—a set of self-limiting, negative beliefs about one's self.

A most critical junction in the psychological development of a child occurs around the age of six years. Before age six a child has no conscious awareness of self. He is not consciously aware of having feelings—they are just experienced internally and openly expressed. Around the sixth year of a child's life there is a significant advance in cognitive development. This change in thinking ability enables a child to be conscious (aware) of his own feelings and basic reasons for them. "I feel happy because Mommy loves me." Or, conversely, "Mommy hurts me, so I must be a bad person." Or, "I am afraid of Daddy." If the child's thoughts about himself are generally and consistently positive, then normal psychological development will proceed. However, consistent realization of negative thoughts and feelings about one's self must be addressed or managed by a child in some way to reduce the psychic pain and confusion experienced. The troubled child has only two options as solutions to his dilemma, and neither one provides a positive outcome.

The first option is to express openly her thoughts and feelings to her primary caregivers, the very people who are the source of her learned negative beliefs about herself. These are the same people she perceives to be all-knowing and all-powerful, the people she depends upon for survival and love. If she risks expressing her true thoughts and feelings, the response from her primary caregivers can range from positive, nourishing responses (which is very unlikely) to ignoring her efforts, dismissing them as ridiculous, or attacking her for being a bad person for thinking such things. This option only leads to worse feelings and thoughts about oneself if the caregivers cannot respond in a healthful manner. More often than not, this is the case .

For example, here is Sara's perception of herself at age six (recalled at age thirty-one):

> I lied to others because I was fearful of not being liked or accepted. I was very angry and confused. I was always afraid my feelings would just be turned around to make me look and feel selfish. I was made to feel guilty for having those feelings. I just needed my mom to hug me and be proud of me. I needed to know I was cared about, just some love, a hug, some support would be nice. Because I believed Mom didn't love me, I thought I was bad. I didn't believe I was worth loving, because I believed most people thought badly of me. I hated my mother and felt sorry for my father, even though he gave me little attention. She was mean to him too. He was gone a lot, and I was left alone with Mom. I learned not to ask her for or need anything. I learned to take care of myself.

The troubled child has only one real option to relieve the internal mental anguish. She must *deny the existence* of the anguish to herself. She must mentally separate from (repress) her real self. She must build a psychic wall between her day-to-day existence and her real, negative beliefs about herself.

Separation from one's real self is chosen out of the necessity for survival, and is the beginning of a divided, conflicted, negative self. It marks the beginning of the slowing or halting of psychological development. This act of blocking awareness of one's self is also the central psychic event that sets the stage for a variety of psychological, emotional, and interpersonal problems in the child's future. The individual's particular expression of psychic dysfunction will be evident by the early teen years. By adulthood, if not before, cutting off from inner truth about one's self leads to a chronic state of poor self-concept, self-distrust, distrust of others, cognitive and emotional confusion, interpersonal conflict, and repeated failure to meet life's challenges or get psychological nourishment.

To have a divided self means that the individual is partially or totally unaware or disconnected from his real Primitive-Self. Unfortunately, denial of one's real self does not lessen its power and control over the individual. Regardless of the disconnection, the Primitive-Self is the individual's dominant force in all thinking processes, such as perception, belief formation, decision making, and behavior. Self-development will be adversely affected by a negative Primitive-Self that is largely or completely unknown to its owner.

The need for psychological survival, and the lack of contact with the real self, focuses the child's priorities for his behavior on the needs of others and on what he must learn to get by. The child has no option but to develop a Surface-Self designed to gain love and approval from others. For this child, unconditional love is absent. In its place is the constant struggle for approval, which is mistakenly seen as love. The child must also create a Surface-Self that protects against awareness of his real self—by anyone, including the child himself. Psychologically the child remains trapped between feeling abandoned and working fruitlessly for genuine love.

Developmental Consequences of a Troubled Primitive-Self

In a psychologically healthy, nurturing environment, the image a child presents to others—his Surface-Self—is an honest reflection of the healthy Primitive-Self that he is continually developing. His Surface-Self is free to express the genuine thoughts and feelings of his thriving Primitive-Self. He is in the process of forming a healthy foundation for development of his Meta-Self that has yet to emerge. As the child develops to maturity, the Meta-Self will gradually assume control of his Surface-Self. In a healthy adult, the Surface-Self displays an accurate representation of the person's Meta-Self.

In an individual with a troubled Primitive-Self, the Surface-Self does not express what the Primitive-Self really thinks and feels; it expresses what the troubled Primitive-Self wants the outside world to know. In addition, a person with a troubled self is not consciously aware of part or all of the content of his Primitive-Self. This disconnection unfortunately allows the troubled Primitive-Self to maintain its dominance, which has the negative consequence of slowing or halting the individual's psychological growth. In fact, the person's disconnection from his real self allows the troubled Primitive-Self to grow in power. Because it is beneath the individual's conscious awareness, he cannot see or understand its negative effect on his life. He is unaware of his impeded ability to grow psychologically. Additionally, with the troubled Primitive-Self in charge of one's mind, the Meta-Self cannot develop. Regardless of chronological age, the person remains a child psychologically, with a negative, immature self concept.

Around the twelfth year of life another cognitive shift advances the child's cognitive ability to see his real self more clearly. If he does not like what he sees in himself, his distress will lead to increased internal confusion about himself. The transition to adulthood is difficult for most adolescents, but it is all but impossible for an individual with a troubled sense of self. Still driven and controlled by his troubled Primitive-Self, the person must face even more difficult challenges in the teen years. With a dominant, negative Primitive-Self, he is ill-equipped to do so. As a consequence, he will begin to act out with dysfunctional behaviors that are a reflection of his inner confusion and distress.

Self-concept formation, for better or worse, is mostly completed by the age of twelve, if not earlier. After age twelve, superficial beliefs about one's self will be affected to some extent by the natural course of events and challenges in life; however, deep-seated beliefs concerning one's self are still dominant. After the self-concept is formed, it will take a conscious and determined effort to cause significant and deep change of the real self for the better. And the longer it takes the individual to own the need for real self-change, the more difficult changing will be.

When it does begin, the goal of changing one's self for the better must center on elimination of the divided, negative self through development of the Meta-Self. To achieve this goal is to become a psychologically healthy adult with *one real and healthy self.* A person governed by his Meta-Self constructively manages his thoughts and feelings with reasoned thinking. With the Meta-Self in control, the individual is able to receive and give nurturance and love. Only through the development of a Meta-Self is one able to know real and functional truth, and achieve all that life has to offer.

A word of caution is in order at this point. While it is true that inadequate parenting is the major cause of most psychological problems, it will do you no good simply to blame your difficulties on your parents and then keep living a life of failure and lack of quality. It is your responsibility, as an adult, to fix what is wrong with you. Don't bother going back to Mom or Dad to tell them what a miserable job they did. They will not remember the past the same way you do. They will not be able to understand your perception. They will not be able to respond to you the way you want and need them to. How can they do now what they were unable to do when you were a child? Whether or not they admit that they were at fault, they will end the discussion by saying, "We did the best we could." You will still be left with the responsibility for changing you.

Signs and Symptoms of a Troubled Self

You may be conflicted about whether this concept of a troubled and divided self really applies to you. Part of you wants to read on because you are getting real answers to questions you have had forever. Another part of you wants to close this book and never open it again. It may be your Primitive-Self that wants you to stop reading, to deny, to discount, to rationalize, and to keep doing what you have always done. Concurrently, the healthy part of your mind, your Meta-Self, may be telling you it's time to take responsibility for what is wrong with you and fix it if you can. Which part of your mind are you going to follow? It's your choice. It's your life.

Following are some of the attitudes about life and behaviors that indicate the need for further self-evaluation:

> » Feeling depressed a lot about life in general

> » Being unable to experience fun or joy in life

> » Living a self-limited existence focused on safety from being hurt

> » Being aware that you are avoiding taking responsibility for doing what is best for you

> » Not having anything you have achieved in life that makes you feel good about you

> » Using alcohol or drugs to make you feel better or escape

> » Choosing to isolate from outside activities and being involved with others

> » Chronically procrastinating about getting started on necessary tasks

> » Not finishing things you start—especially those that would improve your life

> » Having an obsessively fixed routine that causes you anxiety if you have to change it

» Pursuing activities, sports, or exercise excessively as an escape from yourself

» Continuing to do things that your know are harmful or destructive in your life

If any of these attitudes or behaviors describes you, then the knowledge presented in this book is well worth your considered effort. To help with your self-evaluation, Chapter 2 lists many, more specific indicators of a troubled, divided self.

Before proceeding to chapter 2, take time to begin listing your observations about you that are signs of a troubled self. Be sure to allow or require yourself to take responsibility for the ones you usually ignore, discount, and accept as normal because *you* do them.

After you have completed the exercise, proceed to chapter 2 and discover what you have missed in your self-analysis.

•

2

Elements of a Divided, Troubled Self: The Self in Conflict

Beliefs you hold in your mind as truth about you, regardless of how and where they were acquired, compose your reality. These core beliefs are either effective or ineffective in maximizing your ability to meet your emotional needs and achieve your goal of living with the consistent experience of psychological quality.

A Divided, Troubled Self

In a broad sense, the challenge of life is the same for all of us. Our lives are a continuous experiential process of learning about our individual selves and our world. We must grow and change in constructive ways to experience all that is possible within a lifespan. Living is also a constant process of meeting the challenges life places in our paths. For us to realize success and fulfillment, these challenges must be met with knowledge, determination, self-confidence, courage, and competence. What is it that makes this journey through life seem easier and more fulfilling for some, and just a series of painful events and repeated failure for others? Is it bad luck, poverty, ignorance, poor emotional health, or oppression by others that keeps people from the experience of emotional quality in their lives? These factors and others can and do adversely affect our lives. However, there are plenty of individuals who are presented with such obstacles and yet are able to find their way to consistent success, personal happiness, and a fair share of fulfillment in the world.

What elements enable one individual to be happy and fulfilled, while another person continually fails to thrive and feels bad about himself and his life? Good fortune, hard work, college degrees, high incomes, family money, and important friends are of course contributors to success and fulfillment, but there are many people with one or more of these advantages who are still unhappy and unfulfilled. While these elements do play a part in outward success, I believe it is the level of personal *psychological quality* attained by an individual that is at the base of experiencing personal happiness and a fulfilled life.

What you believe and feel about you fundamentally determines how well you fare in life. *What you believe to be the truth about you* influences how you perceive, decide, and approach everyone and everything in your world. If your mind is dominated by negative thoughts (beliefs) about you, others, and the world, it is not a productive and beneficial resource. It is a mind that is at odds with your own well-being, and it is indicative of a divided and troubled self.

Listed below are a few of the internal cognitive and affective indicators of a divided, troubled self:

» Feeling bad about who you are as a person

» Thinking and feeling negatively about yourself, regardless of what you do

» Experiencing confusing and contradictory thoughts and feelings

» Experiencing fear as a constant companion and motivator for actions

» Feeling emotionally immature

» Not actually feeling your own feelings

» Your thinking is often scattered or distracted—focusing is difficult

» Inability to make decisions, especially when strong emotions are aroused

» Not trusting your mind to know what is true

» Feeling empty or valueless inside

» Constantly worrying about whether you are doing the right thing

» Knowing the right thing to do, but refusing to do it

Often, people who have negative self-perceptions are not aware of their real beliefs. Individuals who are cut off from their innermost beliefs about themselves are unhappy, discouraged, and defeated people. They are unknowingly destructive to themselves and to others. They are unable to create or experience nourishing relationships, and they repeatedly behave in ways that reinforce their poor perceptions of themselves. They move through life collecting experiences of disappointment, rejection, and failure without knowing the real cause. People with negative self-perceptions continually search for something outside of themselves to blame, because they cannot or will not take responsibility for their own deficits. Still others unsuccessfully seek something outside of themselves to believe, in order to feel better about who they are. Thus they avoid facing the real issues within themselves.

In many other cases people have at least a partial conscious connection to their real selves and are aware of their negative beliefs and feelings about themselves. The difference is that for these individuals, being aware of a low self-opinion ensures that they will blame *themselves* for their misery—even when they should not. Self-blamers also spend a lot of mental energy believing that others are also seeing them negatively. This is true despite the fact that they try to present themselves in ways that get confirmation or approval from others. They are sure that others see them negatively, because they see themselves negatively. How could anyone see them as anything different? Besides, how can you trust anyone's positive opinion about you when you know they don't see the real you? If they could see the real you, they would not like you. You believe this to be true because you do not like you. Fear of exposure of the real self is a constant companion for these individuals. With time, conscious awareness of their fear is lost, and all that remains is the avoidance of anything that would cause the experience of fear.

People with troubled, divided selves live sad and lonely lives. They live in a solitary place, cut off from outside nourishment and cut off from awareness of their real selves. Consider an analogy of the properties of a thermal container. It has an outer wall (the portion that can be seen and touched), an inner vacuum space of air, and an inner core space for food items. The food items are analogous to the content of a person's real self. The outer wall of the container represents the Surface-Self. This is what the individual presents about the self to others. An individual with a troubled self exists primarily in the vacuum space between the inner and outer walls. The vacuum space represents what the individual is aware of. This portion of his conscious Primitive-Self is at least partially aware of and in touch with the outside world through his Surface-Self. However, his conscious Primitive-Self is cut off from contact with the deepest part of his Primitive-Self, which contains his true beliefs about himself. A life with your mind existing in this vacuum space is a lonesome one. Yet to a person with an impaired sense of self, isolation from his true self and the outside world is the only place for relief and safety from harm. Isolation is a solution for survival that eventually leads to deterioration and self-destruction.

Isolation from other people takes many forms, some of which are easy to observe and others not so readily apparent. If an individual stays by himself in his apartment, rarely coming out, the isolation is obvious. But the individual who isolates while in crowds or while talking directly to you is harder to spot. Isolators are very good at projecting a Surface-Self that looks normal, but looks are often deceiving. People can appear to be listening, but inside they are either preoccupied with themselves or are in a state of mental fogginess or numbness. They may appear to be relating normally, and they may think they are, but in reality they are only acting a part. At the level of their real selves, they know the truth.

Origin of a Troubled Self

An adult person with a divided, troubled self has lived in a state of psychic separation from his real self for many years. Unknowingly, he chose to cut off from his real self at a young age in order to survive psychologically. It was not his fault that he cut off from his real self. He subconsciously chose it as a solution to psychological neglect or abuse and the mental anguish they cause. However, the solution of cutting off knowledge of his real self was not without consequence. The unavoidable result was to create a divided and conflicted mind—a mind that would significantly limit or halt his development toward psychological health and emotional maturity. Despite becoming an adult in years, he has, for all practical purposes, remained a psychologically injured child. He is a child who, by default, learned a belief structure dominated by negative and harmful beliefs about himself and the world in general.

He has lived a life dominated by a Primitive-Self that, early on, allowed him to survive but not to grow as a human being. Now, as an adult, his Primitive-Self dominates his mind with negative, destructive beliefs, of which he is at least partly unaware. He is either partially or significantly disconnected from his real self and lives with conflicting internal realities. He lives with a divided, confused, and contentious self. His thoughts, feelings, and actions are inconsistent, perplexing, irrational, and incongruent. He is not able to trust his own thought processes or feelings to give him valid information about himself or the world. As life progresses he becomes increasingly confused, conflicted, depressed, and destructive. His troubled mind has placed him on a slow but sure path through ever-present suffering, repeated failure, and the absence of fulfillment, and to eventual self-destruction.

A person with a troubled Primitive-Self is dominated by irrational and negative emotions and therefore lacks the ability to think or to act with reasoned self-assurance. Because his mind is dominated by irrational and faulty thinking, he cannot develop faith in his own mind's abilities. A consequence of a lack of faith in one's self is the experience of chronic low self-esteem—the perceived decrease or absence of value as a person. Additionally, because he does not believe in his mind's ability to know truth, he is unable to trust the validity of his mind's processes or conclusions. Consequently he cannot trust himself, nor can he trust his perceptions of others. To be safe, he must always assume negative intent. The end product is a mind that is confused, negative, and self-defeating. It assures its owner consistent failure and unhappiness.

A person ruled by a troubled Primitive-Self, experienced at the most severe levels, must deny the existence of its negative content. He must repress any knowledge of the negative truths he holds about himself. His psychological survival depends on not being aware of his own true condition—a debilitated state of mind generated and sustained entirely by his own negative thoughts and feelings. Such an individual is completely unaware that his own confused and negative mind is his real enemy and that it is he who limits his ability to recognize or experience psychological quality. His true beliefs about who he is, and who he is not, remain totally blocked from conscious awareness. *Yet he is totally controlled by their destructive influence.* If this condition is not resolved, the only possible outcome is the inevitable psychological self-destruction of a human life.

Here is an example of divided and confused thinking:

I often cut off from my feelings when I am in conflict. I don't know how to deal with it other than to cut off and isolate. This doesn't work in my relationships, but I don't know what else to do. I want to feel worthy and valued, to feel loved and be able to give love in return. Why would I want to sabotage myself and my relationships? I hear what you tell me about myself, but even though it makes sense, it's hard to hold on to when I'm not certain on how to convince myself. I can say things to myself all day long. That I'm worthy of love. That I am confident ... etc. But how will I know I actually believe it? Okay, that sounded pathetic. I should be good with telling myself these things and believing them. I believe I'm a nice person. I don't intentionally try and hurt others. I don't steal or do drugs. I live my life the way I feel is right. So how can it be so hard to feel and want good things for myself?

Crystal is conflicted about who she really is. She has a divided self. Crystal is often so overwhelmed with her negative and confused thinking that she shuts off connection with her real feelings and thoughts. She sometimes sees herself as a good person but at the same time is unable to believe that she is worthy of being loved or being happy. In truth she believes both. Her Meta-Self sees her goodness and her real deficits. Her Primitive-Self believes that she lacks value as a person and is therefore unlovable. When she is stressed or threatened, her Primitive-Self reasserts its power and reminds her of her negative self-beliefs. She then isolates and feels bad about herself.

More Signs of a Troubled Self

A troubled, divided Primitive-Self is observable in a variety of signs or indicators. I have given examples of its presence in one's attitude about life and in one's internal thoughts and feelings. The presence of a divided, troubled self is also evident in relationships. The following list presents a few examples:

- » An inability to foster and maintain trust in others

- » Experiencing relationships as primarily troubling and being unable to resolve conflicts

- » Having a history of failed relationships, either because of you or because you chose poorly

- » Often being afraid to express your real thoughts and feelings

- » Constantly being critical of others

- » Unexplained or irrational anger toward others

- » Constantly seeking to gain approval from others in order to feel good about you

» Always trying to please others, often at your own expense

» Avoiding situations where others may say or think something negative about you

» Hiding your real self from others because they won't like the real you

» Feeling emotionally isolated from others while you are in their presence

» Observing yourself lying to others even when it is not necessary

» Not following through on commitments you make to others

» Relying on the beliefs of others, such as authorities, institutions, and traditions, instead of using your own thinking to determine truth

An individual governed by negative primitive thinking and behaving, regardless of actual age, is a person dominated by the ebb and flow of immature emotions. The individual's principal reality is one of cognitive confusion and feeling bad about who he is. On the one hand he may feel that he is a good person, deserving of happiness. At the same time he knows that he feels bad about himself. He may want to be loved but feel undeserving of it. *This dilemma seems unsolvable to him.* Over the years the individual will try many things to resolve his dilemma, but his attempts always fail. His feeling of aloneness and his secret knowledge of his negative self worsen as the years pass.

A person with a troubled, divided self does not realize that his own thinking is the cause of his problems. By the time a person reaches adulthood he is unaware of the deep beliefs that make him feel bad about himself. He is also not aware that only he has the power to change those beliefs that are irrational and harmful. To significantly change his life for the better, he must reconnect with his real self. He must know what he really believes about himself before he can hope to change.

Fear as a Primary Motivator

Perhaps the most prevalent indicator of a troubled, divided self is the presence of fear as the primary motivator in one's life. In the more severe cases, it is the avoidance of the realization of fear. Does fear rule in your life?

- » Are you afraid to ask your boss for a raise?

- » Are you afraid to ask for what you want?

- » Do you avoid confronting your spouse's poor treatment of you?

- » Do you avoid saying what you really think and feel to most or all people?

- » Are you afraid to try new things—especially those that would bring pleasure to you?

- » Do you feel small or anxious around others—your parents, for example?

- » Are you afraid to look in a mirror, into your own eyes?

- » Do you fear making decisions or being wrong if you do?

- » Are you afraid of what others think about you?

If fear is a dominant feature of your life, it is because you are governed by a negative Primitive-Self. The only question is the degree of your disability. Living with fear as a primary motivator limits your options for fulfillment and achievement in life. It wastes energy in nonproductive and destructive ways. The experience of appropriate fear is a part of being human. It is natural and even healthy to have some fear of falling if you are on the edge of a high cliff. It is not natural or healthy to be afraid of saying what you think and feel.

Being excessively afraid is a sign, in fact a billboard, telling you that your development as a person has not been completed. It is saying that you are still controlled by a Primitive-Self that focuses on survival instead of fulfillment and achievement. The rest of your life does not have to be ruled by a fearful Primitive-Self. You can challenge your Primitive-Self to validate being afraid. You can make the decision to stop being afraid. You can choose to change your primary motivator to courage.

Connecting with your Primitive-Self

Here is an example of a journal entry where a woman attempts to get in touch with her Primitive-Self. See if you can identify the underlying core beliefs of her Primitive-Self.

I was a very shy child. I spent a lot of time alone. I think I began to come out of it around the sixth or seventh grade (age twelve). Sixth grade is where I went out for majorettes, but it was hard because it was left up to me to get rides to practice, events, and back home. Nobody in my family came to watch me. My parents had to work all the time. My brother and sister were a lot older and had their own lives.

Around that same time my brother was sent to prison. I was angry at the world and started fighting a lot. It made me feel good to stand up for me. It was also a way for people to leave me alone. I have difficulty trusting people. I learned that you should never tell anything you never want anyone else to know. But I could be loyal and trusted and do anything for someone else. I enjoy doing for others and do not expect anything in return.

I used to believe that if you treated someone a certain way, they would be the same back. I learned the hard way that that wasn't true. It was devastating to me to realize in no way was that true under any circumstances. This was true especially in my marriage. I did everything I could possibly think of to make it work and save it. I was a failure.

After my divorce I seemed to date nothing but losers. They were all selfish, drug users, and self-centered maniacs.

Although my self-esteem is bad, it seems good in some areas. Anything that has to do with my kids' best interest, I have done my best to do. I love them more than I love myself.

I remember my family fought all the time. I was terrified and hid in my room a lot. Whenever my dad was drunk I would go straight to my room and stay there till he went to sleep or left. I learned to avoid him. He would just go into these mad rages for no reason. He was like a ticking time bomb. I used to escape by sneaking out and just walking around for hours. Sometimes I would stay away so long my mother would come looking for me after she came home from work. She knew why I wasn't staying at home. Nobody talked about Dad's behavior or anything else. I had to learn about everything from kids at school. You know, things like monthly periods, hormones, boys, sex. I was always on my own. I know Mom did what she could. She worked all the time to avoid Dad. Dad got worse and worse, I believed that he could kill us at times. He never hit me, but he did hit my mom and my brother. I was always so scared, I just hid in my room or avoided him as much as possible.

—Katie

Katie did a great job of writing openly about her early years. She obviously had a childhood of psychological neglect and abuse. She is in touch with her emotions and is aware of the reasons for them. Despite this awareness of her childhood suffering, she continued into adulthood recreating the same experiences in her marriage, and since then with other relationships. Today, she still has no idea why she is so unhappy and lonely and a failure in relationships, especially with men. She keeps trying and keeps failing. She blames herself, and she blames her failures on having bad luck in choosing men.

Although Katie tried to make her adult life better than her childhood, she remains unsuccessful in relationships because the real cause of her adult failures is unknown to her. Katie cannot see that her negative self-concept and learned ways of relating set her up to fail. She is disconnected from the core beliefs of her Primitive-Self that drive her thinking, feeling, and behavior. Katie has survived on the surface, but she is lonely and discouraged inside. Her solution to her pain has been to work hard and take care of her children. Inside she lives a life of emotional pain and isolation. She has failed to achieve the two goals in life that are the most important to all of us—to have a positive and consistent sense of self and to experience true emotional intimacy with another human being. Her only pleasure in life comes from helping others to experience the happiness she denies herself. In reality, she likely is not providing happiness or emotional security for her children, since she does not have it to give. In the psychological domain, you cannot give a gift you do not possess.

As you can see from Katie's story, if your environment is not psychologically nourishing, your Primitive-Self will not learn to feel good about who you are. Your self-concept will be negative. Your perception of everything will be negatively weighted. Fear and self-doubt will dominate as the primary motivators of everything you think and do. If you were treated badly enough, you will only be partially aware of your own primitive beliefs. But remember that regardless of your level of self-awareness, your Primitive-Self-concept is *who you are* to you. It defines and determines the course and quality of *your very existence as a person.* Any attempted change to this most basic image of self is naturally going to be feared and resisted by your Primitive-Self. To be successful in changing yourself for the better, you must fight through your own Primitive-Self's resistance to change and perceived loss of its control and existence.

A troubled Primitive-Self will endure your surface *behavior* change for a while, but it will not allow deeper and real change as a person. It will tolerate only *attempts* to change. The Primitive-Self will allow you to *try* anything to make you feel better, but it will also sabotage any budding success. Your Primitive-Self, in coalition with your Surface-Self, will find some way to survive, reassert power, and keep control of you—even if it means more pain, suffering, and self-destruction. A troubled Primitive-Self believes that "present suffering is better that the unknown" and that "real change is to be feared because it will mean the loss of who I am." *This internal conflict between the facets of a troubled self happens without the individual's conscious awareness.* Learning to connect with your real self and its struggle is a critical step in the process of change. A conscious connection to your Primitive-Self's beliefs lets you know the content of your resistance to changing.

Struggling with his own resistance to real change, Ted shared the following:

> Oh man, I feel like I just, instead of taking one step backward, I just keep taking more steps backward. I just find myself procrastinating, doing my reading, my writing, just sitting down, and not focusing. I mean that it's on my mind, I just constantly do it, I just I don't know—not sure what all's happening, maybe, I just keep fighting doing it or something. My drinking is another problem. I know I was supposed to stop, but I've only been able to slow it down. I can't get control like I want. I tried to limit it, just like Saturday during the ballgame, that's my Primitive-Self talking, negotiating. That's what it probably was—just another crutch to keep me from doing what I need to do.

Ted's Primitive-Self allows him to *try* to change, but it finds ways to foil his attempts. For real change to occur, Ted must stop using alcohol to escape from his real self. He must find the courage to face it. His confusion is also generated by his Primitive-Self. It distracts him and drains his energy. Ted must learn which facet of his mind is in control of his thinking. He must differentiate between his Primitive, Surface, and Meta selves. He must learn to prioritize and live in his Meta-Self. This is a slow process of trial and error, but with a determined effort, it can be accomplished through hard work.

The Troubled Surface-Self

Because the troubled Primitive-Self cannot survive alone, due to its isolative and destructive nature, it must allow the development of another facet of the mind—the Surface-Self. The Surface-Self's role is to act in collusion with the Primitive-Self. Its mission is to interact with the outside world in order to go on with life and, at the same time, to hide the existence and dominance of the troubled Primitive-Self. This deception is not only directed to the outer world; it is evident in the person's internal lack of knowledge about his real Primitive-Self.

The Surface-Self's mission is to interact with the outside world to gain acceptance, validation, and approval (love). The negative effect of a dominating Primitive-Self is not readily apparent during the childhood years from age six to around twelve. Physical and intellectual development may continue normally through the interaction of the Surface-Self and the outer world. The individual learns to use his Surface-Self in the form of different personas that allow survival and even achievement in the physical and intellectual domains. Signs of a divided, troubled psychological self begin to surface around the age of twelve to thirteen. At this point of life an individual experiences an increase of insight about himself. This is due both to an increase of cognitive self-awareness that is part of normal development and to the increased awareness of internal mental conflict experienced by a troubled individual.

Internal psychological conflicts in the early teen years take many forms. In general terms the individual either will begin to "act out" or will withdraw into his own private world—either path includes a continued disconnection from the individual's real self. Acting-out behavior is, to some extent, normal in teenagers as part of their need to establish a sense of independent identity. Sullenness, arguing, isolating from family, and even doing worse in school are examples of typical behaviors of the teen years. More serious behaviors—excessive truancy, running away, drug and alcohol usage, promiscuity, and prolonged periods of depression or isolation—are more than likely indicators of a divided, troubled self.

Surface-Self personas, at any age, can be seen in many forms, but all are designed to protect a fragile and immature Primitive-Self. What you may think of as a lifestyle choice or eccentricity may be something more. Living in the past, excessive drinking, excessively criticizing others, or compulsive activities are all behavioral adaptations that provide escape from the real self. All of these behaviors serve to distract one's attention and are used to provide immediate relief from internal conflict and suffering.

The Surface-Self does have some healthy, productive adaptations when governed by one's Meta-Self—for example, presenting a neutral face when being criticized by your supervisor, or not telling someone how bad a dress looks on her. These are examples of appropriate insincerity—a beneficial skill.

Primitive-Self and Resistance to Real Change

Inherited characteristics, developmental influences of one's family, and personal life experiences in the world combine to give the individual a unique perception of reality about himself and the world. Beliefs and values formed, particularly in one's early life, guide all subsequent thoughts, feelings, and actions. Once in place, these early learned beliefs are highly resistant to being changed. Research shows that changing deeply held beliefs is resisted because people tend to link comprehension of an idea to believing in it. Once an idea is understood and accepted as true, it is difficult to doubt one's own conclusion. People tend to believe something is true simply because they believe it. Even when presented with rational evidence that contradicts their belief, most will continue to hold on to their original conviction. Once a faulty belief is accepted as true, subsequent information is accepted as true only if it agrees or support beliefs already held as true. Unfortunately this type of unreasoned thinking is prevalent in the majority of people. Unreasoned thinking is a deficit that greatly limits psychological development in a person who experiences a relatively healthy psychological upbringing. However, in an individual who experiences psychological neglect or abuse as a child and is left with a divided and troubled self, a deficit in reasoning ability can be a major block to psychological change for the better.

Once an individual has established a personal set of beliefs about himself, he will resist any attempt by anyone to change the perceived truth. This is true even if the individual wants to change his beliefs and is cooperating. The psychological reason for this resistance is important for the reader to understand, because to enable real change, he must continually challenge and overcome his own resistance to bettering his life. Genuine psychological self-change is resisted because our most fundamental sense of self— what we believe (know) to be true—is the basis of how we define and maintain our sense of existence as well as our perception of ourselves. So, at the deepest level of an individual's mind, attempting to change one's real self is perceived as a threat to actual survival. Most important to the reader's understanding is that the locus of the resistance to change is the Primitive-Self. This part of the self must be dethroned from its power to negatively dominate the course of one's life. The individual must overcome his own Primitive-Self's resistance to experiencing a happier and fulfilling life.

Struggling with her resistance to change, Crystal shared the following:

> I know I isolate too much. I isolate because I know it's my safe place. I know I can't be threatened or have to deal with any conflict of any kind. It's a place that I can be sad and upset, cry my eyes out, or if I just want to be left alone. It's where I can allow myself to be vulnerable to my feelings without anyone knowing. Growing up, there was nobody to go to when I would have a problem or if I was upset, so I learned to deal with things on my own. Nobody else cared. I learned early that I had to take care of me.

Crystal is struggling with the idea of giving up her isolating behavior because it has been her only source of comfort and security. Her Primitive-Self learned at a very young age that nobody cared and that she could trust no one to respond to her emotional needs. Her childhood solution was to isolate and comfort herself.

On the surface she grew up to be a caretaker of others in order to feel needed and loved. But despite all she has given to others, she has never been able to feel good about herself.

Thirty years later, isolation is still her way of existence. To her Primitive-Self, it's better than risking being hurt. She is divorced from a man that confirmed her distrust of others. He was a drug addict and emotionally a child. She has lived the past ten years raising two children alone. She has been through a couple of attempts to have a relationship with a man but never was able to let herself go and trust. She chose poorly in both cases and again had her belief that no one really cares confirmed.

If Crystal is serious about improving the quality of her life, she is going to have to learn to risk trusting others with her real self. She must learn to overcome her fear of being hurt. She must learn to relate to others as a real person instead of relating to others with a Surface-Self that meets their needs at the expense of her own needs.

In Summary

Your Primitive-Self may have helped you survive, but it will not let you grow and change for the better. To improve the psychological quality of your life, you must engage and develop your Meta-Self. Your Meta-Self, the part of your mind that identifies the truth, knows if and why you're unhappy with you and your life, and that change is needed. This is the part of your mind that moved you to buy this and other self-help books, or to seek outside help from a professional helper or other sources.

To your Primitive-Self, real constructive change must be avoided and sabotaged if it is attempted. Remember that change is a threat to your Primitive-Self —a threat to its very existence. It will fight you for its own survival while continuing to make your life miserable with immature and destructive beliefs and behaviors. If left in control, it will lead you down a self-destructive path.

If your Primitive-Self dominates your life, it means that you have not developed the healthy portion of your mind where the Meta-Self is meant to exist. Instead, you are ruled by a Primitive-

Self that impedes your growth and fulfillment in life. Chapter 3 presents and examines the psychological functions of the mind and gives you the opportunity to evaluate whether your mind is working for your best interests or only allowing you to survive while it impedes your growth as a person and creates confusion and continued hardship in your life.

3

Your Mind: Ally or Enemy?

*The value of learning and living truth must
become your most important principle in life.
If you cannot trust your own mind to tell you
the truth, then it is impossible for you to trust
anyone else.*

*Reality is truth, but truth is
not always one's reality.*

The Basic Functions of the Mind

The human mind consists of three basic functions:

» **Thinking:** The thinking or cognitive component of the
mind includes mental actions such as analyzing, comparing,
questioning, and evaluating. Its most critical function is to
constructively think about things to identify truth.

» **Feeling:** The feeling or emotional function of the mind
tells us how we are doing in any given situation or set of
circumstances. It tells us if we are doing well or poorly.
As humans we experience a wide variety of emotions,
from happiness to sadness, excitement to depression, joy
to sorrow, etc.

» **Formation of beliefs:** The third basic function of the mind
is the subjective formation of beliefs, the ideas we *choose* as

truth. Subjective beliefs include things such as values, goals, desires, drives, commitments, and beliefs about everything, including ourselves.

These three basic functions of our minds are interactive and interdependent, meaning that each function influences the others in reciprocal ways. When thinking occurs, some related feeling and belief is always involved. However, despite the fact that all three are important functions of the mind, *thinking is the mind's most important function.* If you want to change a feeling, you must identify the thinking that leads to or causes it. If you want to change a belief, you must identify the thinking that drives it. It is thinking that leads us to take any action or avoid any action.

In a psychologically healthy person, the thinking portion of the mind is highly developed. The principal element in a healthy person's mind is its ability for rational, reflective thinking—the capacity to use reasoned thinking as a guiding force over the other two functions of the mind, feeling and the formation of beliefs.

Thinking, Feeling, and Acting—a Microcosm of Life

Thinking, feeling, and behavior do not occur independently of each other. They are all interrelated and interdependent. A particular thought causes one to feel a certain way and then to behave in a certain way in response. That behavior then triggers the next thought—and so on.

Thought————Feeling————Behavior————
New Thought————New Feeling————, etc.

This process can also occur solely at a thinking level, where each thought causes feelings and then the feelings generate new thoughts. In this case, new thoughts are cognitive behaviors.

Thought————Feeling————New Thought————
Feeling————New Thought————etc.

Recognizing this causal relationship among thought, feeling, and behavior is critical to understanding objective and reasoned thinking. All thoughts, feelings, and behaviors are interdependent. For example, a person cannot experience a feeling without *first* having a thought that causes it. Another way to say the same thing is that there are always reasons for feelings. To assess the soundness of your thinking, you must identify what you are feeling, identify the thought (or thoughts) that caused it, and evaluate them as a unit for rationality. A rational thought leads to a rational feeling and then to rational behavior. An irrational thought leads to an irrational feeling and to irrational behavior.

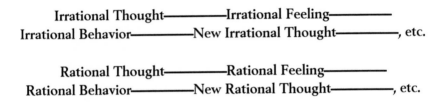

Rational thinking, feeling, and the resulting behavior are products of one's Meta-Self. In less healthy individuals, emotions are irrational responses, driven and dominated by the irrational thinking of a Primitive-Self. Irrational thinking generates emotions that are distorted, immature, extreme, inconsistent, or contradictory (incongruent). Often an individual is only aware of surface emotions, such as being confused, angry, or depressed, and has little or no connection to deeper, more significant, and real feelings in his Primitive-Self. In the most severe cases, complete emotional disconnection is evident. The individual has learned to numb his awareness of all emotions, positive and negative.

Thinking versus Feeling?

Is it better to be a "thinking-centered" person, or is it better to be a "feeling-centered" person? Everyone seems to have an opinion, and their choice of which is better is biased according to how they perceive themselves. In reality, people hold many *mistaken beliefs* about the relationship between thinking and feeling. To believe in any of these erroneous beliefs is an impediment to any self-change effort. Read the following list of commonly held mistaken beliefs to see if you accept any of them as "fact" or simply "feel" they are true.

» Thinking and emotions are not compatible with each other

» Thinking-centered people are cold and lack compassion

» It's possible to feel without thinking

» It's possible to think without feeling

» It's perfectly healthy to be an emotional person and do little reasoning

» It's perfectly healthy to be a rational person and experience little emotion

» My emotions should always guide my thinking

» You have to give up a rich emotional life to be a rational-thinking person

» You must give up being a rational-thinking person to value feelings

If you agree with any of these mistaken beliefs, think twice. Read the statement again to see if you understood its meaning. Now, if you still believe the statement true, you probably have a bias about that particular belief. Perhaps it's a long-held belief that you have just taken for granted as true without ever seriously considering its merits. Keep thinking and talking about it until you can understand why it is false. Holding on to mistaken beliefs will obstruct your ability to grow psychologically.

Remember, to be mentally healthy, you must believe in and master the *integration* of the thinking and feeling functions of your mind. Thinking always underlies your experience of emotion, and in turn, emotions drive your thinking. Healthy thinking requires the rational inclusion of emotion. To accomplish this necessary integration of the functions of your mind, it is imperative that you improve your ability to guide your thinking and feeling with objective reasoning—reasoned thinking.

Feelings—a Dubious Source for Truth

Emotions (feelings) play a major role in human life. They define us as human beings and help us to experience life, as we know it. If our minds work effectively, feelings help us understand ourselves and connect in meaningful ways with others. For example, the human ability to experience the feeling of love is, to my way of thinking, the most beneficial feeling and value we humans have. We believe in love. We practice it. We are nourished by it. That is the good news.

We also have issues or problems with love. We love something or someone who is not good for us or does not love us in return. We fail in loving others by not demonstrating it when or how we should. We are afraid to love, because we might be hurt by the risk. We love an idea, so we kill those who do not love the same idea, or who hold an opposing, threatening idea as truth. And worst of all, too many of us fail at loving ourselves. As you can see, love can be a positive, beneficial emotion, or it can be negative and destructive.

On an individual level, many people believe that their emotions represent truth simply because they experience (*feel*) them. They believe that the act of feeling an emotion *makes it true*. If you believe that your feelings are always truth and that others should accept them as valid and be responsive to them, then I would bet that your life is one filled with constant disappointment, if not disaster. If this sounds like you, perhaps it's time to reevaluate how to make feelings a more constructive part of your life. This can only be accomplished by incorporating reasoning into your thinking. The facet of your mind where more constructive thinking is learned is your Meta-Self.

The Meta-Self's capacity to manage your emotions is a learned process of integrating the experience of emotions with reasoned thinking. For example, experiencing (feeling) an emotion *makes it real to you*. However, experiencing a feeling as real does not mean it is also a valid *functional* feeling. The functionality of a feeling is indicated when it is rational, accurate, and beneficial.

In reality, feelings are subjective responses to your known and unknown subjective thoughts. Therefore, they are better initially viewed as subjective facts, consequences of thinking, which should be considered as subject to error, and therefore must be evaluated and guided by reasoned thinking.

In a psychologically healthy person, feelings are *consciously* experienced (felt), coupled with a causal explanation, and evaluated for functional validity and appropriate expression. This means they are consciously owned as real but not accepted as being functionally valid until they are assessed for causal reason, rationality, meaning, intent, and then appropriate expression.

If you are living with a troubled, divided self, your feelings are driven by primitive, immature, and irrational thinking and feeling. Primitive-Self thinking is dominated by irrational feelings of fear, hurt, and anger. Reasoning is not part of the thought processes of a Primitive-Self. Thinking is limited to experiencing negative thoughts and feelings, escaping from negative feelings, and hiding one's real self from discovery.

Unreasoned Thinking

All people think—for better or worse. It is the quality of thinking that matters.

Despite the fact that humans all have the capacity for learning to think with reason, most have not developed the ability. Instead, most people's thinking is belief-centered and therefore biased. They do, however, believe that they use reasoning to support their beliefs, if they think it's necessary. The discrepancy in their thinking begins with their definition of reasoning. In fact, most people have no idea what reasoned thinking is. The following are examples of *mistaken* perceptions of reasoning:

» Reasoning is simply "having reasons" for what they believe and do. (They may or may not be aware of their reasons.)

» Reasoning is the act of "being reasonable" (meaning that they think they are aware of other views on a particular issue, but listening, understanding, or considering the validity of other views is not necessary).

» Being "reasonable" is conforming to rules, traditions, or accepted procedures—just accepting what has already been decided as truth. This, of course, is something they agree with.

» Valid reasoning is whatever they think, feel, or do just because they think, feel, or do it.

» Reasoning and being calm and logical are the same.

These typical definitions of "reasoning" are actually all examples of its opposite—of biased or faulty thinking. Faulty thinking is invalid or irrational thinking that causes the thinker to arrive at the wrong conclusion.

Irrational thinking is also when, for no rational reason, someone takes a position in spite of conclusive evidence to the contrary. This type of irrational thinking is emotion-driven and involves denying reality. Because the nature of denial is to be unaware of what is being denied, it is difficult to catch yourself. You may have to rely on a friend who seems wiser to show you the inconsistencies or fallacies in your thinking, in order to learn to catch yourself.

Psychologically, irrational thinking is a state of mind that is significantly limiting and harmful to the individual. An irrational thinker believes he knows the truth but never evaluates the validity of his thought processes. He has learned to ignore his own faulty and often contradictory thinking. To support his beliefs, he selectively chooses only facts that support his opinions. He may or may not be aware of this behavior.

In the psychological realm, irrational, unreasoned thinking is always a major feature of individuals with acute or chronic emotional or psychological problems. In the case of acute crisis, unreasoned thinking can be a temporary condition that ends or at least lessens as the crisis dissipates. In people with chronic (long-term) psychological issues, unreasoned thinking is a dominant and debilitating part of their illness and their lives.

By the way, you can be a person who has a deficit in reasoned thinking and still be at least a fairly healthy person. If so, you will just continue to feel justified with your opinions and annoy those that attempt to reason with you.

At this point in the discussion, you may still be wondering if you are a reasoning thinker or an unreasoning thinker, and whether it is affecting your psychological health and fulfillment. To help you decide, here is a list of symptoms that indicate harmful, unreasoned thinking. If you have any of these symptoms, you might want to consider looking for an underlying problem within yourself:

>> Not trusting your own judgment about yourself and others

>> Having trouble making decisions

>> Knowing that some of your beliefs are contradictory

>> Letting your feelings dominate or direct your thinking

>> Being annoyed by people who sound confident to you

>> Having a propensity to adopt the beliefs of others

>> Changing what you believe often, or not being sure of what you believe

>> Sensing that other people's opinions seem better than yours

>> Not knowing how to challenge the opinions of others

>> Tending to think fact by fact and have trouble seeing the big picture

>> Observing that you are rarely sought out for advice

>> Finding that your opinions are often seen as black and white, all or nothing in character

>> Knowing that it is difficult for you to figure out how to do things, even with directions

>> Believing that "logic" is a foreign or a dirty word

» Not relating well with people who "think too much"

» Having trouble understanding or seeing riddles or puns as humorous

Valuing Reasoning

If you are like most people, what you were probably taught as a child is that feelings and logical, reasoned thinking are completely different and at odds with each other. Typically, little boys are taught to value and practice *logical thinking* and especially to value facts. Conversely, little girls are taught to value their *feelings* and the feelings of others as the source of truth. In reality, both logical thinking and emotions are necessary for valid, beneficial thinking for both men and women—and either one alone is ineffective. As you may have learned in life, valuing either one to the exclusion of the other causes problems. Mental health and interpersonal competency require that you learn to value, understand, and integrate both perspectives. Attaining this balance is accomplished only by improving your ability to incorporate reasoned thinking as the guiding force in your thought processes.

Reasoned thinking combines emotional experience with objective thinking. It must be learned through focused practice of the rules and methods of logic and reasoning. This is the same way you learn any life skill. For example, you learned to drive an automobile by learning the rules and skills through focused practice. Learning to think rationally and more objectively is accomplished the same way. Learning to think rationally is, however, more important than learning to drive an automobile, because the quality of your experience of life depends upon it.

In addition to reading this book, it would be wise to spend some time and energy learning about reasoned or logical thinking, especially if you were not taught to value it. Buy a book on basic logical thinking. Knowledge of logic and reasoning will make you better at evaluating your own thinking and more effective at understanding and responding to the people you care about. Suggestions for such reading may be found in Appendix B.

If you were taught to value *unemotional* thinking and facts over letting your emotion guide you, you may be better than others at reasoning, *or you may not be.* Knowing and reciting facts is not the same thing as reasoning. Facts are just one ingredient in the reasoning process, and facts can be chosen in a biased manner. Learning to reason effectively requires you to be aware of and consider *all of the relevant facts*—not just the ones that agree with your opinion. In addition, as almost any woman can tell you, emotions are important to the person experiencing them. You cannot discount anyone's emotions and hope to relate well with them. Connecting with your own emotions and the emotions of others is an important ability in any situation, and especially in relationships. By the way, if you see yourself as a logical, fact-based individual, it may help you to view feelings as *subjective facts*—facts about a person's emotional state. Subjective facts must be addressed in order to make progress and are therefore relevant to any discussion and to reaching a mutually agreed-upon solution.

A Primer on Truth

The goal of reasoned thinking is the identification of subjective truth that is functional and beneficial. But the concept of "truth" is just as diversely defined as "reasoning." Many people believe that there can be many truths about the same thing, and some people believe that truth does not even exist. In my way of thinking, truth is important; in fact, it is vital. If I cannot trust my mind to tell me what is real or true in a given situation, I'm going to have problems.

It's therefore important that you understand what I mean when I talk about the importance of knowing and living truth, and that you understand the different types of truth that affect our lives on a daily basis.

Trusting your mind to know truth cannot be taken for granted. What if you're wrong? Let's begin your learning about truth by exploring its nature and looking at typical processes people use to identify it.

Truth can be divided into two kinds: objective truth and subjective truth. Objective truths are few in number and are absolutes.

They are simply reality, and no alternative to their existence as truth is possible. They are self-evident. A person's very existence and the fact that he will die are examples of absolute truths. Objective truth is only a very small portion of what people live as truth. The majority of truths we identify and live are subjective truths—*man-made* truth. Man-made truth is only what someone decides it is. It is conceived subjectively through thinking and choosing what to believe. In the psychological realm of human existence, we are concerned with the *quality of subjective truth*. Subjective truth is good in the psychological realm only if it is functionally valid and beneficial to a person's well-being. In other words, does it work, and is it good for a person's mental health and growth as a human being? An obvious example of a beneficial subjective truth is universal agreement that it is wrong to murder. Another example is the beneficial practice of adopting and following traffic laws.

For an individual to be mentally healthy and experience psychological quality, his truths must enhance his existence constructively without impeding his mental health and psychological development.

You may be saying to yourself, "Truth is a difficult, if not an impossible, thing to know. Who am I to presume to know truth? What makes this author think he knows what truth is?" These are fair questions. My answer is that you are looking for answers, and you have come to me for them. Listen to what I have to say, and you decide if it makes sense to you. It's your responsibility to decide what truth is. If what I am presenting does not make sense, reject it and keep looking.

Determining truth is something we all attempt to do every day of our lives, but our efforts can be for better or worse, depending on the quality of our thinking. The saying "Garbage in, garbage out" applies. Poor thinking produces poor conclusions. Faulty (irrational) thinking results in faulty conclusions. Thinking negatively about your self, coupled with a lack of reasoning, invariably leads to erroneous, irrational, and destructive conclusions about what is true.

Common sense tells you that not everything believed to be true is true. This is easier to observe in other people's behavior. If you are self-aware, then your own experience is full of examples where you were certain something was true and later found out you were wrong. In fact, we are all wrong about something almost daily. We tend to discount or ignore this fact. People who are mentally sound pay attention to their thinking and behavioral mistakes and learn from them. People who are less than healthy repeat the same mistakes again and again.

It should also be obvious that people generally disagree about almost everything. Can they all be right? On the other hand, millions of people may believe something is true. If many people believe that something is true, does that always mean it must be true? People used to believe that the world was flat. People also believed that the moon was a god or was made of cheese, or that man could never travel to its surface. Historically men and women have been burned at the stake because others believed them to be wizards or witches. Man's history is filled with examples of mistaken beliefs. The fact that many people believe something to be true is not a sound basis for accepting it as so.

On an individual level, and contrary to popular opinion, the act of simply believing something is not sufficient grounds for its validity. To be mentally healthy you must have an effective method for determining truth and a standard for assessing the validity of your thinking. As humans, our only means of determining functional, constructive truth is reasoning. Subjectively perceived truth must hold up to reasoned evaluation as being rational, functional, and beneficial. Truth that is constructively beneficial is based upon reasoned thinking—never on subjective emotions or simply desiring it to be true.

Mentally healthy living requires identifying and accepting reality and seeking functional truth through reasoned thinking in all areas of one's life. *Reasoned thinking is the pursuit of subjective truth that is functional and beneficial.* "Functional" means that it provides workable and beneficial meaning and performance in the individual's life. Functional truth that is determined through reasoned thinking is not psychologically limiting, harmful, or destructive. It is beneficial to the individual's growth as a person and to his quest for value and fulfillment in life.

What is the source of your truth? Too often people decide to accept something as true simply because they *want it to be true.* Other times something is assumed to be true because they have *always thought it so.* Still other truths are accepted because *they come from someone of authority or perceived expertise.*

In fact, you are reading my book because you perceive me as an authority and are looking for some new, helpful truths. How are you going to decide, among all the truths I am presenting, which ones are valid? Are you consciously aware of the mental processes you employ to decide truth? Following are typical examples of attitudes and behaviors about truth.

People believe something to be true because they ...

> »   want to believe it

> »   are used to being told what to believe

> »   perceive that it agrees with something they already believe

> »   "feel" that it is true

> »   hear it in a way to make it true

> »   refuse to hear what they do not want to believe

> »   are unable to separate what is relevant from what is irrelevant

> »   are unwilling to explore an idea thoroughly and tend to oversimplify

Tom is an example of a person with a troubled and divided self looking for truth:

I have been staying busy practically around the clock lately to keep my mind off our current family situation (Dad having left Mom). It was the last thing on earth I would have ever expected my dad to do. He has left all household responsibilities that my mom cannot take care of to me. To this day he has not mentioned one word about this matter to my sister. The only way my sister knows is from what she hears from Mom and me. My dad is that ashamed! He has got to be miserable. I realize I am twenty-eight years old, but my family was so close, and it has been really hard, and it doesn't matter how old you are. I think if I were in his shoes, I would want to do anything possible to make my family happy, no matter how I felt. I know you and I do not agree on this matter, but I just do not see myself having a relationship with him unless he makes things right with his family. He has been an embarrassment, and he certainly still has a chance to make things right if his family is of any importance.

Tom is very upset that his parents are separated. He hears only what he wants to hear—what he needs to hear to support his own perception of how things should be. He blames everything on his father, because he is the one who initiated the marital split. Tom doesn't care about the reasons for his dad leaving; he is only concerned with his own need for his family to remain intact. He projects his own feelings of shame and fear onto his father and concludes that his father feels miserable about himself. (In reality, his father is relieved to have finally found the courage to leave.) Tom thinks his dad should do whatever he has to do to keep everyone else in the family happy, with no regard for himself. It's Tom's way or nothing. He refuses to listen to his father's reasons for leaving, because whatever they are, they go against what Tom believes to be true, to support his own self-centered needs. For Tom, truth is what his immature Primitive-Self needs it to be, in spite of reality.

Identifying Truth through Reasoned Thinking

Feeling good about who you are and being able to find fulfillment and experience a life of psychological quality is dependent on your ability to have faith in the workings of your mind. When you have trust in your mind, you know what is real and what is false. You know what is beneficial for you. You know what is harmful. You have faith in your ability to learn anything you need to know to make your life better. Your mind is your ally. It provides you with truth and direction. Because it knows constructive, beneficial truth, it both guides you and holds you accountable for staying the course. It is your advocate. It is not your enemy.

How do you currently decide what is right or wrong or what is true or false? What is your mind's method or system? Are you even aware of it? Do you just assume you know what is true? Everyone must make decisions regarding truth hundreds of times every day. What time should I get up? What should I eat for lunch? Was Tom lying to me? How much of this medicine should I take? Why do I put off exercising when I know I should? Who is the best person to vote for? Why did my husband leave me? What will happen to me after I die? These are all questions that require you to identify constructive truth. And in every case, the truth you choose will be for better or worse in that it is either accurate or inaccurate and beneficial or harmful to you or others. It is your responsibility to make constructive and beneficial choices. Remember too that all of your choices lead to consequences, and they, too, are your responsibility.

An individual with a divided, troubled self has learned to avoid, deny, and distort truth. He therefore cannot make sound, beneficial choices. He is not guided by truth, reality, or reasoned thinking. I am always reminded of the Primitive-Self when I think of Jack Nicholson's character in the movie *A Few Good Men*. His famous line was "You can't handle the truth!" A person who lives life dominated by a troubled Primitive-Self is a person not willing or able to deal with truth. For an individual with a troubled, divided self, truth (reality) changes with the moment-to- moment experience of primitive emotions and with the perceived immediate needs of the Primitive-Self. To a troubled Primitive-Self, acceptable truth is limited to irrational choices that prioritize safety and not being discovered. By the way, it was Jack Nicholson who could not handle any truth that challenged what he already believed.

For a troubled Primitive-Self, truth is also living in a constant state of fear and cognitive confusion. At an early age, the individual with a troubled Primitive-Self chose isolation from the outside world, and from the truth about himself. It was the only solution to the experience of confusion and bad feelings about himself. Developmentally, the cost of hiding from truth, the reality of oneself, is the failure to grow in a psychologically healthy manner and to achieve emotional maturity. The afflicted individual will continue to develop physically and may grow a significant amount intellectually, but psychological development will be significantly limited or absent. The ultimate cost of being psychologically impaired early in life is a future filled with disappointment, failure, and for many, psychological self-destruction.

A mind that distorts or denies truth cannot build self-efficacy: faith in one's mind to know truth. Because an individual with a troubled self denies truth, he is unable to identify what is true, even when he wants to. He cannot judge what is true about his self or others. As a result, his troubled Primitive-Self lives in a fearful state of cognitive and emotional confusion—at odds with and cut off from his real self. A person with a mind that cannot recognize truth cannot trust his own judgment and therefore cannot develop faith in himself. Because life requires us to make judgments, regardless of the quality of our thinking, the troubled person makes judgments that are self-limiting, irrational, and harmful to himself and others.

A person with a troubled, divided mind must seek relief and resolution from constant and pervasive confusion and failure. He may look for something outside of himself to believe in that will provide him structure and emotional support. He may choose to live in isolation from others, either physical or emotional, to be safe from harm. Or he may seek constant confirmation and reassurance about his self by being a pleaser of others. His attempts to feel good about himself will be in vain. Outward attempts will fail because an individual governed by a divided and troubled mind does not trust his mind to know in whom or what he should place his trust. Therefore, internally, he experiences a vicious cycle of attempting to get confirmation by trusting others and failing to do so.

Outside attempts to reassure or comfort the individual fall on deaf ears because his mind cannot recognize and trust its own processes and conclusions, and he never knows what is valid. Even positive and valid feedback is rejected, because the individual *knows* his real self and *knows* he does not let that real self be seen. He believes that his real self would be rejected. After all, he dislikes his real self, so how could anyone else value it? Life is experienced as one failure after another to find acceptance, understanding, reassurance, and fulfillment for a troubled self. As the years pass, ever-increasing psychic confusion, suffering, and failure become the dominate state of the person's internal existence. Escape from one's self and isolation from others provide temporary relief but are destructive solutions that only lead to increased dysfunction and destruction.

Is it possible to reverse this crippling and self-destructive process? Yes, but it will take major mental reconstruction to change the course and quality of the individual's life. The individual must develop the portion of his or her mind that has been neglected—the Meta-Self.

In a person with a mind dominated by a troubled, divided Primitive-Self, the Meta-Self has remained in an underdeveloped state. The mind's function of finding and applying functional truth never develops. Instead, the Meta-Self exists as an inactive, powerless element in a mind dominated by irrational and destructive primitive beliefs. Changing one's life for the better requires the awakening and developing of the power and abilities that can only be established within one's Meta-Self.

Developing your Meta-Self begins with the conscious choice and commitment to identify, value, and *actually live* functional, beneficial truth. Seeking and living constructive truth requires you to challenge the validity of everything you have previously learned about yourself and the world—without exception. Everything you have learned must be reevaluated to determine if it is rational, constructive truth. If what you believe to be truth is not rational, valid, and beneficial, it is to be discarded in favor of something better. Then, as you discover constructive truth, you must hold yourself accountable for living it in all areas of your life. Learning and living constructive, beneficial truth must become your most important principle in life. This is meta-principle number one. (See chapter 6.)

You may still be wondering why knowing and living truth is so critical. (This is your Primitive-Self resisting.) Ask yourself how long you could function or even survive without knowing what is true (real) and what is false. For example, how can you change a belief in your mind that is harmful and destructive if you do not know what that belief is? It is impossible to evaluate and change a faulty belief of which you are unaware. Knowing the truth about your current beliefs, especially about you, is the only way to effect real change for the better in your life. Additionally, your ability to determine truth about your own inner experience and belief structure determines the level of your ability to discern truth externally, in everyday life.

In Summary

The perception and validation of beneficial truth is dependent on the learned ability to think with reasoning. Although all humans are born with the *capacity* for reasoned thinking, it is not automatic. The ability to think objectively (without bias) and reason is a learned skill, and the ability to learn it depends on the individual's level of maturity plus his level of acquired mental health. The information presented in this book is only an introduction to reasoned thinking. As stated previously, you should devote time to finding other sources about logic and reasoning. Finally, don't just assume your reasoning skills are adequate; you may be wrong.

Psychological growth to maturity and a stable, positive experience of one's self are results of a lifetime of quality thinking. Mental illness, emotional problems, and interpersonal difficulties are results of a lifetime of irrational or invalid thinking.

Quality thinking begins with deciding to seek truth through reasoned thinking. It requires taking conscious control of one's thought and feeling processes. Conscious control entails searching for objective and subjective facts that logically support any idea, opinion, or feeling you believe to be true about anything, especially yourself. Thinking with reasoning also requires looking for new facts that may logically dispute what you believe, and being open to change should those facts make better sense.

Constructive thinking is the responsibility of the individual. Truth through reasoned thinking must be valued over previous learning, myth, unexamined feelings, tradition, and the opinions of others, including experts and external authorities. Any proposed truth must hold up to reasoning and lead to constructive behavior. If any two proposed truths do not agree and support each other, then at least one of them is invalid. Beliefs held as truth must not be contradictory—they must be congruent.

The psychological quality of your life is profoundly affected by your deepest beliefs about you and the resulting quality of your thought content and processes. What you believe to be the truth about you influences how you perceive, decide, and approach everyone and everything in your life.

In essence, your mind is either your ally, or it is your enemy. If your mind is your ally, you have the capacity to identify functional truth; it is an asset to creating quality thinking, good judgment, and interpersonal competence and fulfillment. You may be critical of your thinking or behavior at times, but your focus will be on solving and correcting your mistakes. If you have learned to reason adequately and incorporate the importance of valuing emotions in the thought process, then you are probably fairly competent in identifying functional subjective truth for any given situation. You are your own best advocate and the best source for beneficial truth to guide you through life. You have faith in your mind and in yourself.

Your mind is your enemy if it is divided and in conflict with itself. Having a mind that is divided means that your mind works against you and your best interest. It does not provide you with rational, constructive truth or direction. It is driven by a Primitive-Self that is only focused on reinforcing and maintaining the negative status quo. Much of what you believe is irrational, invalid, and harmful to you and others. You will fail to thrive, mature psychologically, or find nourishment in relationships or fulfillment in life. You will remain a person dominated by a Primitive-Self.

Real change begins with the desire for and the discovery of the content of your deepest beliefs about you. You must know what you believe to be true about you, in order to know what you need to change. Once you are connected with your real beliefs about you, then you can begin the process of developing constructive, beneficial beliefs that will change the course and quality of your life. You can begin building your Meta-Self.

4

The Meta-Self

*Take ownership of who you are
and who you will become.*

Sound Thinking and Faulty Thinking

Our minds are always active. We are all always thinking and feeling, but our thinking and the resulting feelings and actions are for better or worse. Your thinking can be either beneficial or harmful to you and others. How *well* you think—the level of your ability to use your mind effectively—determines the quality of your thinking. By the quality of one's thinking, I mean its soundness, rationality, and functionality. Are your thought processes and the resulting content of your thinking beneficial to your life? Does your thinking impede or enhance your psychological health? Do you think negatively about yourself, others, and life in general? *Fundamentally, the quality of your thinking determines the quality of your life.*

There is a broad range of thinking practices, from irrational, destructive thinking to rational, healthful thinking. Irrational or faulty thinking of any type is destructive because it leads to the formation of false beliefs and harmful behaviors. In my experience, too many people, regardless of their state of mental health, are unaware of the fundamental beliefs they hold in their minds as truth, that both define them as people and direct their thinking, feeling, and behavior. In many cases, people are consciously aware of some of their core beliefs but do not know how they adversely affect their behavior. Additionally, they are unaware of the contradictions that exist among the beliefs that they hold. Their thinking is superficial and biased, focusing on immediate, self-serving needs and desires. Their ethics are therefore situational. They ignore facts that disagree with their beliefs and refuse to own or even consider their faulty thinking and actions.

A mentally healthy adult is governed by his Meta-Self and is consciously aware of what he believes. His thinking is directed by reasoning, and his chosen beliefs are in agreement with reality and are rational, ethical, and beneficial to him and others. A person governed by his Meta-Self is consciously connected to all of the beliefs held at all levels of his thinking. He is attuned to how they are expressed in his behavior and holds himself accountable for their *functional soundness and agreement.*

Trust and Self-Efficacy

Throughout adulthood, all human beings, regardless of the quality of their thinking or their level of mental health, seek to fulfill two universal psychological goals. The first and foremost fundamental goal of all humans is to think and feel good about who they are as individuals. Every individual wants to be able to look in the mirror and see someone he likes and values. He also wants to be someone others can like, love, and trust. He wants to see himself as a good person who is happy, self-secure, and successful, and as one who brings happiness to others. Everyone wants a *positive self-concept.*

The second universal goal of all people is to find at least one other person with whom to share the experience of true emotional intimacy. By intimacy, I do not mean just the physical act of sex. The act of sex can be a physical expression of genuine intimacy, but it can also just be a physical act and therefore not real intimacy. True psychological intimacy actually encompasses a much larger and deeper spectrum of experience. To experience psychological intimacy is to allow your real self to be visible and therefore vulnerable to another person. In response, the other person must see, accept, and value the real you. In relationships, the experience of genuine intimacy is a two-way street. Both individuals must risk communicating their real selves. The psychological experience of true intimacy is to feel valued and loved for the whole of the real you, including your innermost self, warts and all. If, in response, you receive understanding, acceptance, and perhaps love, the relationship deepens. However, while love (romance) is an important element in the experience of intimacy, it is trust and respect held mutually that makes relationships both fulfilling and lasting.

Trusting others with your real self is only possible to the extent that an individual has learned to know, trust, and value his real self. To achieve the universal life goals of a positive self-concept and the experience of true intimacy, you must be able to trust your mind to know truth and make sound decisions. To trust the capabilities of your own mind is to have self-efficacy. A person with a high degree of self-efficacy trusts in his mind's ability to reason effectively and to identify truth.

Trusting your mind's capabilities enables you to make sense of your own thoughts and feelings as well as events in the outside world. Because you trust the processes of your mind, you are able to observe events objectively and then analyze and organize relevant facts with which to form rational opinions. You are capable of recognizing relationships among events, extracting accurate meaning, and applying the information to specific behaviors such as decision making and relating functionally with others. Only by activating and developing your Meta-Self will you be capable of experiencing self-efficacy.

The Meta-Self

The Meta-Self is the portion of the mind that is reasonably objective, responsible, appropriately mature, and able to reason to identify functional and beneficial truth. It is my considered belief that all people possess a Meta-Self; however, far too many have not developed it to the point where it is the guiding force in their lives. When the Meta-Self is underdeveloped, thinking is dominated by the Primitive-Self. The result is a mind that is ruled by immature and irrational beliefs, faulty thinking, and harmful and destructive behavior. It is a mind motivated by fear and focused only on survival and not growth—a mind that ensures repeated failure. A person with an underdeveloped Meta-Self, a dominating Primitive-Self, and a misdirected Surface-Self will find it impossible to obtain psychological nourishment. The inevitable result is the failure to grow to psychological maturity, leading to eventual discouragement, emotional isolation, and self-destruction.

So what do I mean when I say that a mentally healthy person is one who lives in his Meta-Self? First and foremost, it is the healthy adult self, the Meta-Self, that knows truth. Further, it is the Meta-Self that values the reality-based principles of identifying and living functional or workable truth and employing reasoned thinking as the only means to identify it. The primary goals of the Meta-Self are to build and maintain faith in one's self and in one's ability to succeed in life. Having faith in yourself is to value who you are and trust in your own mind. Trust in one's self becomes the basis of trusting and loving others and of being able to be loved.

Living in your Meta-Self and experiencing consistent psychological quality requires always being aware of reality (truth) within yourself and acting based on what you value, as much as you are able, in the external world. Living in reality means using one's mind to identify what is functionally true in any situation. "Functional truth" is defined as truth that is reasoned to be rationally conceived, functionally valid, and not harmful to anyone, especially you.

While it is true that you cannot discover absolute truth for every situation, you can and must arrive at functional truth that is constructive within a particular context and responsive (beneficial) to your nature and needs. You must employ the skills of reasoning to identify functional truth. If you make a wrong decision, then you must learn from that mistake and choose better the next time.

A common trait of mentally healthy people is that they know their growth and success in life depend on accepting what is real without attempting to distort it to fit what they might wish it to be. In all areas of life, a mentally healthy individual makes a consistent effort to see and understand the best workable truth for any given situation and strives to hold himself accountable for actually living that truth.

A common trait of unhealthy, irrational thinkers is distorting truth and being unaware that they are doing it. Distorting truth is a form of rationalizing employed by the Primitive-Self to keep or reassert power over an individual who is attempting to grow. Catching this regressive behavior will be difficult until you have developed a Meta-Self to the point where you are better able to distinguish its thought processes from that of your Primitive-Self. Learning to discriminate between the facets of your self will take time and a lot of effort, and journaling is critical to the success of this endeavor. (See chapter 5.) When you write in your journal, you are writing to you about you. Your goal is to consciously connect with the real you. To do so you must be thinking in your Meta-Self yet observing your Primitive-Self, the facet of your mind that holds your real beliefs about you. Journaling is a concrete means to hold you accountable for going to that part of your mind. It is too easy to fool yourself if you rely solely on thinking and avoid writing. Putting your thinking down on paper makes you connect concretely with your thoughts and take responsibility for them. You will be forced to confront the truth and functionality of your beliefs. By the way, your Primitive-Self will try to convince you otherwise. It does not want to be discovered. Overrule your Primitive-Self's efforts to dissuade you, and do the work.

Cognitively (internally), living truth means choosing to think in your Meta-Self and require it to govern your behavior. This requires having a conscious connection with one's real self from the perspective of the Meta-Self, and constructively managing the integration of current and past thoughts, feelings, and actions. Accordingly, all currently held beliefs—and resulting values held as truth and guiding principles—must be based on the accurate perception of reality and sound reasoning. All beliefs held as truth must also be congruent (in agreement) with each other and consistently *lived*.

Behaviorally (externally), living truth entails being your real and healthy Meta-Self in your interactions with the external world. Internal thoughts (beliefs) must be reflected in Surface-Self behaviors, and these actions must be based on and compatible with functional reality. Being functionally compatible does not mean that you must seek approval from others or that you have to always conform to what others deem acceptable. However, it does mean that you must be able to present yourself in a manner that is not grossly detrimental to your own well-being. A psychologically healthy person values and lives in reality and learns to constructively interact with society, yet he remains, to some extent, psychologically independent of its limiting and destructive beliefs.

Consider, for example, that we are all expected to accept authority, conform to the lifestyle and beliefs of those who came before us, and accept, as truth, information presented by experts, celebrities, religious leaders, etc. As children we are taught to accept what others define as truth, even when it is obviously contradictory to other so-called truths being taught. For example, your religion may have taught you that you were born a sinner and, at the same time, that you are a good person. How can you be both? You were taught not to question the contradiction. You were taught to just accept its irrational nature and told you were just unable to understand. We are taught that because we are children, we are unable to know truth, and therefore we must just accept and not think about that which we cannot understand.

In the family and in the larger community, acceptance and love is granted to those who abide by others' conceptions of truth and do not challenge obvious faulty thinking and the resulting faulty beliefs. By the time people reach adulthood, most have accepted these faulty and harmful beliefs as reality. It is the rare person who is able to break with childhood learning and learn to think rationally about what he learned as truth. To be a truly healthy psychological adult, you must do exactly that. You must develop both a Meta-Self and the ability to identify and live rational, reality-based truth. To be a psychologically healthy individual, you must be able to use your own mind to judge what is true and make all of those truths compatible and supportive of each other. If you do not or cannot achieve this ability, then psychologically independent thinking and higher levels of mental health cannot be realized.

Meta-Self Characteristics

A person governed by his Meta-Self is …

» consciously connected to all facets of his self and in constructive control of his thinking, feeling, and actions

» always responsible and self-accountable for and to himself—physically, intellectually, and psychologically

» focused on reality—identifying and accepting objective and functional truth, and living it

» committed to growth as a human being, to the limit of his personal potential

» proactive in holding himself accountable for initiating beneficial, constructive thinking and actions

» empathically connected to himself and others, with a focus on genuineness, respect, understanding, and constructive action

To live in your Meta-Self means that you value truth over myth, previous learning, tradition, the status quo, or opinions of prevailing authority. You hold yourself accountable for identifying and living truth that is functionally valid and noncontradictory. Remember, functional truth can be either objective or functionally subjective, in that it holds up to reasoned analysis and leads to productive, beneficial results—psychological well-being, interpersonal competence, and fulfillment of your potential as a human being.

In summary, the Meta-Self is the healthy and mature facet of your mind that knows truth—the truth about who you really are and who you are not. Your Meta-Self knows right from wrong, functional from dysfunctional, and beneficial from harmful or destructive. The Meta-Self identifies and solves. Its values are, after all, identification of truth through reasoned thinking and beneficial growth of the individual. Irrational thinking and continued suffering with no real solution or learning is unacceptable.

The choice to live in one's Meta-Self is a choice to value, seek, and live functional and beneficial truth. It is a mentally healthy person's goal to seek truth through the constructive use of his mind. An individual whose thinking is directed by his Meta-Self manages his needs and desires constructively. He seeks objective truth about himself and evaluates the validity of his perceptions concerning himself and the world. He knows his personal growth and success in life depend on it. He works to identify what is real without attempting to distort it to fit what he might wish it to be. Through consistent, focused effort, he strives to understand and accept objective reality; and where given the option, he chooses the most functional and beneficial subjective reality his reasoned thinking can discern.

Here are some examples of individuals learning about their real selves and working to establish their Meta-Self perspectives. The first is Penny, speaking about her initial connection to her Meta-Self:

I'm doing the right thing by making myself write. I need to read more also. I feel good that I've really noticed how uncommitted to myself I have been, despite myself, despite considering myself as a person loyal to others. I am loyal, just not to me. But now I've noticed that I feel committed to noticing myself and acknowledging me and wanting to do more for me. Time will just have to pass to show me how committed I stay to myself. I just don't know what to do, other than reminding myself to push through those fears of stepping out of my security zone. Whenever I feel hesitant I need to ask myself why. I just don't know what to do when I don't have an answer. I guess I need to be more vigilant of myself, so when I don't have an answer, I can remember to ask you. Maybe I can find answers myself, too. I know we have talked about this focus on my self in the past, but it's just starting to click. I guess I was lacking the concept of being vigilant of myself. I have to watch myself and observe myself like a child right now. It sounds silly, but it sounds like the responsible thing to do. The other night I talked about how I've avoided responsibility, in particularly the responsibility of participating in life. I don't respect that about me, and I don't want to not respect myself. So I have no choice but to start being responsible so I can earn my own respect and develop into the person and adult I feel good about."

Penny has just realized the importance of being her own self-advocate. It is her responsibility to herself to hold herself accountable for becoming someone whom she values. She doesn't have all the answers yet, but she realizes it's her responsibility to find them and incorporate them into her life. She realizes that she must replace fear as her major motivator. She must adopt courage to challenge everything she is afraid of in life. She has already begun to display courage by owning the truth about her real self.

In writing from the perspective of her Meta-Self she has also discovered that she must be vigilant of herself. She is responsible for who she is and who she wants to become. She must, in fact, learn to parent herself. She must learn to live in her Meta-Self so that she can build respect for who she is.

Joe's story is that of a Meta-Self in action:

I was just as nervous going into this talk with Dad as the previous conversation. "I'm nervous. I'm not used to this kind of exposure in our relationship. Do you feel it too?" I then got right into the "big three"—Dad's overly critical approach, his being coercive, and his use of guilt. I left him no way of dodging what I was saying. He didn't say anything, just looked at me and nodded. It was about seven to ten seconds of silence but not an uncomfortable silence for me. It was a relieving silence. I finally achieved immediacy in my relationship with my dad. I also challenged my fear of doing it. I broke the silence by saying I don't appreciate his use of these tactics in our relationship. I assured him that I was not there to beat him up over the way he treats me but rather to notify him that moving forward, I will be pointing out to him when he is treating me in a way I don't deserve.

Joe demonstrates thinking driven by his Meta-Self. His account of his conversation demonstrates both clear thinking and assertiveness for his rights in the relationship. He is demanding respect from his father for the first time. This took courage and faith in his ability to express his thoughts and feelings with power and yet demonstrate consideration for his father's value as a person, even though he was critical of his behavior—the very thing his father had never done with him. In the next example, Joe demonstrates his Meta-Self managing his Primitive-Self's attempt to take power.

> The talk with Dad and my getting new golf clubs have really stirred up my Primitive-Self. As soon as my clubs arrived I started feeling anxious, childish, and small—like I don't deserve to talk to my dad like that and I should feel guilty for having these new clubs and leaving work early to try them out. Strange dreams last night too. One where I was constantly battling bad guys (aliens, animals, ghosts) and another reoccurring dream where I am trying to tee up a golf ball to hit it, but I can't ever find the right spot, don't have room for a backswing, the ball keeps falling off the tee, and the tee disappears or turns to dust. This all happens while other people are watching me, waiting on me with critical impatience.

Joe demonstrates his conscious connection with his Primitive-Self from the perspective of his Meta-Self. Joe's Primitive-Self is trying to reassert power by reminding him of how he has always doubted his own thinking and how little he used to value himself. It is also saying that the old beliefs are still true. Joe must mentally reassert his new beliefs about himself in response to his Primitive-Self. He must do this repeatedly until he solidifies faith in his Meta-Self's ability to govern his thinking and behavior effectively and consistently.

Here, Lauren is learning to observe her Primitive-Self and distinguish it from her Meta-Self:

> What a fool I have been. I'm finally getting a different per-

spective on myself, my husband, and my marriage. I hope it's from my Meta-Self. Is anger legitimate in the Meta-Self? Anyway, I spent twenty-five years with that man, raising our children, even working outside the home for the last ten years to supplement his loss of income. I have done everything to make *him* happy, always doing things his way, even many times when I knew better. He has always had everything his way, even back before we were together. I know this because his family still protects him from any responsibility, especially being at fault for anything.

I think that I have figured out why he wants to divorce me after all these years. Plain and simple, *I had the audacity to grow up and expect something in return from him.* The marriage was fine (for him) for the first fifteen years or so. And I guess it was okay for me too. I was busy rearing children and being the good wife. Our trouble started about twelve years ago when I had to get a job to help with our finances. I began to learn that I was pretty smart, with a good head for business and a way with people. I started feeling better about me and growing as a person. George was fine with me working and bringing in extra money, but gradually he grew dissatisfied because I had to spend more and more time at work, because I kept advancing. The more I worked, the more unhappy he became. His needs were less and less attended to in his mind. In reality I worked hard to do both.

I guess I learned that I had value when I went to work. I enjoyed it, and I felt nourished by the experience. Two years ago when George shocked me by asking for a divorce, I was terribly hurt. I thought he loved me. I didn't know what I had done wrong. When I pushed him to tell me why, all he said was, "You're just not the girl I married anymore."

For the last two years I have pleaded with him to reconsider and work with me to save our marriage. All he does is blame me. I'm tired of being blamed, but I bounce back and forth between feeling guilty about changing from the "girl" he married, and not trying hard enough to meet his needs, and getting angry because my needs for a husband to value and love me were always missing. Don't I have a right to be loved? I'm sick of feeling guilty, of being confused, of trying to please him even though he is the one who wants to abandon me.

I guess the bottom line is that he doesn't like me anymore because I have changed over the last twelve years into someone who is somehow a threat to him. I am becoming an adult. I have become a woman who has rights and needs. I'm seeing clearer now, and what I see is that George just is not able to meet my needs and is unwilling to try. He still wants everything his way. I just need to let go.

Lauren does a great job of looking at herself more objectively from the perspective of her Meta-Self. She sees how divided and troubled her thinking has been over the years. She is tired of blaming herself for doing nothing worse than growing up and asking her husband to give her what she has given him. In a later journal entry, after she is clearer about her negative, self-defeating, Primitive-Self beliefs, she turns them into goals and challenges herself to accomplish them:

I know that I need to set a self-development goal so that I have a clear picture of who I want to be. My goal is to be a functional and self-secure adult governed by my Meta-Self. To succeed in accomplishing this goal I must focus all my attention on me, not on my relationship with anyone else. I think it will take me at least a full year to accomplish this goal. So, I'm going to get started today. My Meta-Self says I will know I have reached my goal …

» When I am in good company when I am alone,

» When I am not only my best critic but also my best advocate,

» When I am anxiety-free, both alone and with others,

» When I can put meeting my own needs in a relationship on an equal footing with the needs of my mate,

» When I am strong enough to be my real self and choose my friends because they know, accept, and like the real me,

» When I can express what I really think and feel to others and believe I have the right to do so,

» When I am able to take responsibility for what I do that is right or wrong, and when I can also give responsibility to others when they deserve it, and

» When I am able to expect to get the things I need from my mate, whoever he may be, the things that I am willing and able to give. These include empathy, respect, genuineness, commitment, caring, acceptance, and love.

Lauren is determined to learn to develop and live in her Meta-Self. She is structuring a program to hold herself consciously accountable for reaching a specific goal and has specified who she will be and what she will be able to do when she has achieved it. Once her goal is achieved, she will have established some very strong and healthy principles for living and relating in the future.

Developing Conscious Principles in your Meta-Self

To be successful in building, maintaining, and living in your Meta-Self, it is necessary to develop a conscious set of valid and beneficial principles to govern your thought processes and actions. These principles are in fact a new set of positive, valid, and productive beliefs about you and the world. These new beliefs are the mental building blocks that will determine your new values. You will also need to consider how you will hold yourself accountable for actually living them. The meta-principles you adopt will form a foundational set of beliefs to build a mature and psychologically healthy life.

The development of your Meta-Self principles requires the acquisition of new knowledge and the conscious assessment and restructuring of your current beliefs. Any proposed change of a current belief must meet the standards of being reality-based, rational, and constructively beneficial. If a new belief meets these standards, it should be incorporated into your mind as a meta-principle. Proposed beliefs that are not compatible with reality, or prove irrational or harmful to you or others, are to be rejected.

People who are psychologically responsible, mentally healthy, and appropriately mature for their particular age have a set of conscious meta-principles that guide them successfully through life. These principles are fluid as opposed to static in nature. This means that principles can change with new learning, but they must always be rationally conceived, functionally valid, and beneficial to the psychological well-being of the individual. As an individual gains mastery in living a life directed by his Meta-Self, his meta-principles will become more refined and stable.

Although there is fluidity in adapting meta-principles to new experience, there are three absolute and unchanging meta-principles that are universal in application and fundamental to all other beneficial principles and values. They will not change with time or new experiences.

Universal Meta-Principles

» To know, value, and live in functional reality (truth)

» To know, value, and live conscious, constructive, reasoned thinking

» To know, value, and live a lifestyle of psychological growth

Living Meta-Self Principles and Values

If you are thinking with your Meta-Self, you know right from wrong, and you know what to do in most situations you may encounter. When you do not know what to do, you will do your best to gather the facts needed to make the right decision. When thinking in the Meta-Self, you do not stay confused or overwhelmed by any problem or emotional state. You do not give in to negative and irrational thoughts or emotions. You use reasoning to identify new truth and determine the validity of new ideas and resulting emotions. You choose objective, reality-based thinking to guide your course of action. And you evaluate your choices with the same process.

Remember, *you cannot just think* about what is more functional and healthy. *You must actually live* in your Meta-Self to learn to be a healthy person. To have faith in yourself, you must exercise your psychic meta-muscles to strengthen your Meta-Self. This *must be a continuous, conscious effort.* In the beginning of the process of change, you must identify the characteristics and beliefs of a mentally healthy person and how they are displayed in thinking and action. What are the principles that guide healthy people? You will find them through your own productive thinking, through reading, and by observing others. As you identify healthy principles and values, your challenge is to incorporate them into your principles and hold yourself accountable for living them.

Meta-Self Skills: Empathy

Empathy is the ability to *communicate* that you are listening and understanding another person's perception of his own experience. Empathy is a learned interpersonal skill that is based on and reflects the individual's level of mental health, and his ability to be aware of his own true thoughts, feelings, and actions. You cannot communicate empathetically with others to any degree beyond the level of awareness and objective insight you have of yourself.

The level of internal empathy you have is proportional to the level of conscious connection you have with your real self and the degree that you have developed your Meta-Self as the dominant source of your thinking. An individual with a divided, troubled self has little empathic ability because he lives with a Primitive-Self that limits or denies conscious connection with his real self. If you are not connected to your own real feelings and beliefs about you, then you will be unable to identify and connect with the emotional experience of others. A troubled Primitive-Self will not let you connect with others, because to do so would connect you with your real and negative Primitive-Self. In addition, If you are even partially connected to your real Primitive-Self, but your thoughts and feelings about you are primarily negative, the nature of your beliefs will prevent empathy for others. You will be too preoccupied with your own suffering to have any concern for others.

In order to build the power of your Meta-Self and become more psychologically healthy, you must hold yourself accountable for risking connecting with others empathetically. The internal result will be resistance generated by your Primitive-Self. This resistance is an opportunity to connect with thought processes and beliefs of your Primitive-Self and counter its negative content with constructive content from your Meta-Self. The more you challenge the negative power of your Primitive-Self, the faster growth will occur.

Following are a few cognitive questions to help you in connecting empathetically with yourself and with others:

- » What is she really feeling right now?

- » What is she really saying that she wants me to hear?

- » What is her intent or goal in talking with me?

- » How is she feeling about me right now?

- » What is she thinking about me?

- » What am I feeling right now?

- » What is the real reason for my feeling?

- » Am I in my Primitive-Self, Surface-Self, or Meta-Self right now?

- » What is my Meta-Self's perspective of this person and this situation?

- » How will she interpret what I am going to say, from her frame of reference?

There is another important reason to develop your capacity for empathy. Empathic ability is the fundamental ingredient in being able to establish, experience, and maintain emotional intimacy. *Without empathy, true intimacy is impossible.*

The Meta-Self in Relationships

Individuals who have developed themselves in a healthful psychological manner to the point of being governed by a strong Meta-Self live in relationships differently than others. People who value themselves and are responsive to the rights and needs of others have high expectations of themselves and those with whom they relate. They are "givers" in relationships, as opposed to being "takers." They have learned a valuable lesson: the more you give to others, the more you get in return. Their giving, though, is not unconditional; they expect it to be reciprocal.

Believing you have the right and the responsibility to have expectations in a relationship, and having a clear understanding about what you legitimately need and desire in any relationship, gives you the confidence to express those rights and expectations and hold others accountable for meeting them. For example, in choosing a mate, you should be clear on the traits and behaviors that are a must for you. You should also know the qualities that you would like to have in a mate but would be willing to compromise on because they are of less importance. Physical attractiveness or beauty may be one of these to consider. Remember, in the long run, the ability to trust and respect someone is more important than physical beauty. On the other hand, there is no substitute for chemistry. Attempting to compromise too much and force yourself to focus solely on internal character will not work either.

In Summary

Experiencing psychological quality in your life is both an immediate goal and a lifelong process of committed growth as a human being. It is a continuous quest for faith in one's self through self-awareness, self-understanding, self-acceptance, and self-directed change. Learning to engage and develop one's Meta-Self is the only way to accomplish these goals. It is only by building the power of the Meta-Self that you will be able to feel good about who you are.

The journey of positive change entails a difficult process of identifying the self-limiting and self-defeating beliefs of one's Primitive-Self, from the perspective of the Meta-Self, and then facing the task of learning to be in good company when you are with your real self. It requires employing the Meta-Self's perspective to identify, adopt, and actually live new, constructive beliefs as conscious principles for governing your thinking and behavior. Meeting the challenge of positive change also requires an attitude of openness, a resolve to consider new knowledge and skills, and the courage and determination to incorporate the changes that will surely follow.

A mentally healthy person is one who lives fully in his Meta-Self. The Meta-Self is distinguished from the other facets primarily by its capacity for reasoned thinking. The ability to reason enables an individual to manage the integration of his emotions with reasoned thinking to identify functional truth, the most important element in establishing and maintaining mental health, fulfillment throughout life, and continued psychological growth.

5

The Process of Changing Your Self

*Be patient with you, the person, but persistent
with your determination to change.*

You might be asking yourself, "Why do I have to uncover all these bad things that are going to make me feel worse about me?" This is a Primitive-Self question. A healthy Meta-Self would reply, "The reason is simple. You cannot change what you are unaware of." Are you afraid to know the real you? What you do not consciously know about yourself *can* hurt you. Make a Meta-Self decision to be courageous and discover the real you. The parts you like, you can keep. The parts that are harmful are within your power to change. Your future is in your hands—or rather, in your mind.

Make a Commitment to Real Change

In my clinical practice, many people have come to see me to resolve problems and find solutions that inevitably involve making changes in themselves. They come to me and other helpers because their way of making sense of the world has failed. They cannot help themselves. They need new answers and solutions. I have never kept statistics, but only about half of the people who come to see me remain in treatment with me for more than three sessions. Some of these go on to seek treatment elsewhere, but most just go back to their lives without treatment. They were either unwilling or unable to proceed.

From my perspective, to make real change a reality, people

85

must be both *willing and able* to do the work required to improve the quality of their lives significantly. They must have a strong desire for change that is born from consistent failure, and they must have some level of a rational and positive sense of self that they are able to build upon. It is also evident that many individuals are willing to do whatever it takes to change their lives but are unable to accomplish the task without help. If this proves to be true for you, I have provided some direction for finding effective outside help at a later point in this book.

Real psychological change requires changing your innermost core beliefs, the beliefs that define you as a person—to you. These deeply held beliefs are difficult to change. First and foremost, you must really *want* to change your life for the better, and then you must work diligently to accomplish it. For real and lasting change to occur, you will need to work persistently to identify the core beliefs that make up the real you, evaluate their functionality in your life, and replace the beliefs that are limiting or harmful to your mental health and growth as a person.

Step number one in this process is to establish a conscious connection with your real inner self—your troubled Primitive-Self. For most people, this step is the most difficult because of the resistance your own mind will naturally generate. What is it resisting? It is resisting change to the status quo—the way things are now. The human mind resists change for two reasons. The first is simply because your mind's long-held beliefs are familiar, and therefore everything is understandable and predictable. To a troubled mind, present pain and suffering is predictable and is therefore preferable to the unknown. The idea of changing one's beliefs, especially about one's self, invokes fear—fear of the truth, because it may be worse than the present pain. The second reason people resist real change is that the deepest beliefs we hold about the self define who we are as people and are therefore tied to our definition of existence—even if those beliefs are harmful to us.

It may seem irrational that a person in real crisis would resist help and a chance for real, constructive change. You are right: it is irrational as well as self-destructive. But the fact remains that the more troubled and divided the self is, the more resistance it will generate. The more troubled a person is, the more the denial and disconnection from the real self will be evident. In more severe cases there is complete separation from the real self. As you attempt to make changes in your long-held beliefs, do *not underestimate the power of your own resistance to discovering the real you. Expect it, and find ways to get through the persistent roadblocks your Primitive-Self will generate.*

Now you know what you're up against—yourself. You must overcome your Primitive-Self's opposition to being exposed and changed. Begin your efforts to connect with your real self by owning your unhappiness—your negative thoughts and feelings about you and your experience of life. Next you must take responsibility for being the only one who can make your life better. Once you have accepted the reality of your troubled self and acknowledged your need and desire for change, you are ready to begin the process of connecting to your real self. To begin this introspective journey, you must activate your Meta-Self. In doing so, you begin the process of developing the power of your Meta-Self and also initiate learning how to live with it in charge of your life. You begin living meta-value number one: Seek and live functional truth.

Seek and Live Truth

Seeking and living functional truth begins with discovering the truth about what *you really believe* to be the truth about you, as a person. If you have a divided, troubled self, much of what you will discover will be negative. This is to be expected, because you obviously have negative beliefs about yourself, *because* you are troubled. *(If you do not agree with that last statement, it means you are still blaming others for your problems and your Primitive-Self is resisting quite well. Go back and read chapter 2 again.)*

Be advised, your negative self-beliefs were learned in early childhood and are deeply ingrained as part of your identity. These beliefs are the default thinking content of your Primitive-Self. If you are going to improve the quality of your life, it will be necessary to reprogram your troubled mind. This reprogramming can only be accomplished by activating and developing you Meta-Self—the part of your mind that knows and values beneficial truth.

You are perhaps at least partially aware of your core negative beliefs about you, but you just don't know what to do about them. For example, you may be aware of some recurring negative thoughts about yourself, and you are probably aware of your history of disappointments and failures. What you are not aware of are the deepest self-beliefs that drive your negative experience of yourself. These are the core beliefs about you that control everything you think and do.

You have tried everything in your power to fix the problems you have experienced in your life. And if you are like most people, you have tried to resolve your problems by every means except owning and changing your real inner self. You have tried to change your surface behavior, changed jobs, changed relationships, made more money, stayed busier, invented distractions, and gone to church more, and nothing has worked to make you feel better about you.

To achieve real and lasting change, you must identify the real problem within you before real success is possible. The real problem lies in your deepest perceptions of yourself. To quote the cartoon character Pogo, "We have met the enemy and he is us." Or, to paraphrase Pogo, "I have seen my enemy, and it is my self."

As explored in an earlier chapter, your real problems originated in your early learned beliefs that reside in your Primitive-Self. Once you became aware of those negative beliefs about you, you denied their existence and did the best a child could do to go on with life. In a regrettable paradox, the more the beliefs of a troubled Primitive-Self are ignored, the more they dominate your life. Remember, if your Primitive-Self is troubled, its primary goal is *only* survival. Therefore, its mission will be to generate resistance to discovery, and to any change initiated in your newly established Meta-Self. You must repeatedly identify your Primitive-Self's attempts to resist change and defeat its destructive efforts. (Yes, I'm being repetitive.)

Changing yourself is a process of trial and error, of success and setbacks. It is moving ahead by initiating new beliefs and behaviors, and temporarily reverting to dysfunctional thoughts and behaviors. Don't believe your Primitive-Self when it tells you that you are different and therefore do not have to worry about relapsing. *Expect and own these relapses as quickly as possible, and learn from them.* Keep moving forward toward building your Meta-Self and a new you. Be patient with you, the person, *but be persistent with your determination to change.*

Learning to Identify the Facets of One's Self

In order to build a healthy, adult Meta-Self, you must learn to discriminate between the facets of your self. "Which part of my mind is doing the thinking at this moment? Am I thinking in my Primitive-Self, my Surface-Self, or my Meta-Self?" Learning to distinguish which part of your mind is in control at any given moment will be a difficult task in the beginning, because your Meta-Self is underdeveloped, and therefore your Primitive-Self will be more powerful. Be wary—your Primitive-Self will always be ready with new ways to fool you. For example, you may believe that you are thinking with your Meta-Self when you are not. With consistent effort, you will develop your Meta-Self's abilities and become quite proficient in objectively discerning the source of your thinking. As a beginning, in learning to detect which facet of your mind is in control, you can ask yourself, "Which part of my mind is in control of my thinking at this moment? Is it my Primitive-Self or my Meta-Self?" If your thoughts are negative, you are more than likely in your Primitive-Self. If your thinking is positive, you are most likely to be in your Meta-Self. Here are the major differences between Primitive-Self and Meta-Self thinking:

- » Your Primitive-Self practices confused, foggy, or scattered thinking.

- » Your Meta-Self is clearly focused and refuses to remain confused, foggy, or scattered.

- » Your Primitive-Self is motivated by fear and avoids discovery and change.

» Your Meta-Self is motivated by courage and actively seeks truth about your self.

» Your Primitive-Self thinks in negative terms and makes you feel bad about you.

» Your Meta-Self may be critical of your behavior but is always your advocate.

» Your Primitive-Self thinks negatively and irrationally and suffers.

» Your Meta-Self thinks positively and rationally and seeks solutions.

» Your Primitive-Self thinks immaturely and is driven by emotion.

» Your Meta-Self thinks maturely and is reasoning-focused and more objective.

» Your Primitive-Self's goal is to keep your life as it is, even though it is miserable.

» Your Meta-Self's goal is to make your life a pleasant, even joyous, experience.

» Your Primitive-Self does not solve problems in ways that are beneficial to your mental health and growth as a person.

» Your Meta-Self holds you accountable for doing what's best for you and what makes you feel good about being you.

Penny's journal entry (Week 10) is an example of an individual's efforts to connect with her real self and learn to discriminate between the facets of her mind.

Who is the real me, and what are the feelings that define me? What are the reasons behind those feelings? From where I stand now, I feel superficial and sort of vacant when I try to know the real me. I know substance is there, but I just can't pin down what it is. I'm scattered, but I'm kind. I'm flaky, but I have good intentions. I'm lazy, but I get things done. I'm curious. I'm observant of others. I'm playful but feel bad because I'm having fun. I feel like I don't deserve fun, because I'm not doing important things, like reading, as much as I should be. I always feel like there's never enough time. I feel rushed, which in turn makes me slow down, and then I feel lazy, which makes me feel overwhelmed. I still don't know the reasons behind these feelings, and I stated all these feelings in relation to myself—not in relation to anyone else. I guess I don't know what it means to be real. I don't know what it feels like to judge whether or not I'm really being real. I'm just confused again.

Penny is struggling to know her real self. To this point, she has been able to connect with many of her true feelings and reasons for them; however, she is unable to discriminate between her Primitive-Self, her Surface-Self, and her Meta-Self. The result is confusion. The confusion is generated by her Primitive-Self. Her statements show some real insight about herself, but she must learn to separate healthy self-beliefs from negative, primitive beliefs. Her statements about herself are unclear and contradictory, self-flattering and self-critical. They are positive and negative at the same time. In mathematics, a positive times a negative is always a negative. The same is true for Penny. Her negative statements about herself always trump the positive ones. The harder she tries to sort them out, the more confused she gets. In the end, she is back to not liking who she is and separating from her real self.

Penny's challenge is to break down her perceptions of herself into simple "feeling and reason" statements. In doing so, she will move toward discriminating which facet of her mind is generating which feelings and the specific reasons for them. *She must be in her Meta-Self to perform this task.*

Here are some feelings and reasons expressed or implied by Penny in her journal entry: *uncertain, unclear, superficial, vacant, frustrated, scattered, flaky, well-intended, lazy, curious, observant, playful, bad, undeserving, hurried, rushed, overwhelmed, and confused.*

Here are some of her simple feeling and reason statements:

"I feel bad when I'm having fun, because I'm not really supposed to have fun." (Primitive-Self)

"I feel scattered inside, because I cannot decide what to really believe." (Meta-Self)

"I feel bad, because I'm not reading as much as I should be." (Primitive-Self)

Notice how the Primitive-Self's statements are critical, negative, and in one case obviously irrational. Its goal is to survive and maintain control of your thinking. Its method is to keep you focused on feeling bad about you.

Once you have some success at thinking in your Meta-Self and making accurate observations about which portion of your mind is in control of your thinking, you will begin to feel the difference that healthy thinking makes in your life. The following exercises and activities will facilitate your learning to adopt a Meta-Self thinking perspective. To successfully use the information gained from your "feeling and reason" work in order to isolate the core beliefs of your Primitive-Self, your Meta-Self will need to be in control. You must know the core beliefs about your deepest self before real and lasting change can occur.

Time Out

Pause for a few moments in your reading for a short exercise designed to help you to focus on the real you. As you learned in primary school, adjectives are words that describe nouns—for example, a *yellow* bird or a *quiet* mouse. Think about adjectives that describe you. Make a list of ten adjectives that best describe you—the real you, as a person. Be careful to avoid listing adjectives that other people use to describe you. *Only your real beliefs about you are important.* Also avoid adjectives that describe who you *want* to be or who you *should* be. Connect with your real, private self, and be honest about your beliefs. *Do this now before reading any further.*

After listing the ten descriptive adjectives, number them. Number 1 will be the adjective that describes your real self the most, and number 10 will be the adjective that, on this list, describes you the least.

After you have completed the exercise ask yourself the following:

» How many of the words you have chosen are negative?

» What does that say to you about you?

» Do you like the person you see as you?

» Are you your own self-advocate?

» Which of the words are really feelings?

» How would you summarize your own description of you?

» What did you learn about you?

I hope you took your time with the exercise. Be sure to write all of your information about you in your journal. It will provide a good starting point for your future conversations with yourself about you.

Connecting with Your Real Self

The goals of these next exercises are to help you connect with your real self and to help you identify your Primitive-Self's core beliefs. The exercises include work in ...

1. Monitoring your feeling experiences,

2. Building a feeling-word vocabulary,

3. Journaling to you about you,

4. Identifying core beliefs, and

5. Observing and responding to feelings and reasons observed in others.

These exercises are just a few of the effective ways to help you to connect with your real self. Think of other means to uncover your true beliefs—for example, looking at childhood pictures may kindle memories of events that you have forgotten. Or talk to your older relatives who knew you as a child and perhaps have a clearer perspective of your early life.

Monitoring Your Feeling Experiences

Your emotions are your doorway to the truth.

Human beings are constantly experiencing emotions in response to all types of stimuli; however, people with troubled, divided selves are largely unaware of this constant stream of emotions. Long ago they subconsciously decided that it was better not to be aware of their negative feelings and the negative thoughts that cause them. Instead they block all strong emotions, positive and negative, or they avoid feeling altogether.

The essential first step in real self-change is establishing a *conscious* connection with your emotions. Your emotions are your doorway to the truth. To begin, get in the practice of monitoring and identifying your feelings during your waking hours. Record your feelings, as you become aware of them, in a small pocket notebook. Consciously attempt the experience of really *feeling* and naming your feelings. Then, if possible, write down the reason for each feeling.

You will probably need some kind of key to remind you to focus on your feelings, because your Primitive-Self is going to try to make you forget, be too busy, or invent some distraction. Placing a sticky note on your rear-view mirror, carrying a notebook, or writing an *F* on the palm of your hand are ways to help you remember. You can think of others. *The important thing is for you to hold yourself accountable for doing this work.* Your goal is to restore your awareness of your own emotions. Later, when you are writing in your journal, your goal will be to recall these feelings, reexperience them, and begin to identify the reason or reasons that explain each feeling. Remember, your feelings are the doorway to your real beliefs about you, and when they are coupled with their reasons, they provide you with the information needed to uncover your deepest core beliefs.

Building a Feeling-Word Vocabulary

You must actually feel your feelings
to make real progress.

Another exercise that will help you connect with your real self is collecting new feeling words and ideas from sources other than yourself. The process of collecting feeling words will help you to connect with your own feelings and give you new feelings to explore. Don't forget that when you are doing your feeling work, it is imperative that you actually *feel* your feelings, not just think them. By allowing yourself to really feel your emotions, you open the pathway to your real self. Learn to listen to your thoughts as you search for feelings in yourself and in your observations of others. This exercise may seem simple at first glance, but for many people who have spent most of their lives disconnected from their real selves, it will be difficult and may even be frightening. Remember, you must challenge your fear at every opportunity. Don't give in to it. You can only learn to be courageous by deciding to be courageous.

Where do you search for feeling words? You observe your own experience of yourself and your thoughts about anything, and you observe the behavior of people all around you. Remember, feelings are being expressed by everyone all the time. A word of caution is in order: be careful not to approach this only as an intellectual exercise, or that is exactly what it will be. You will have missed its real purpose—to connect you to you. *Feel* your feelings, and identify the real reasons for them. *Identifying your real feelings, feeling them, and knowing the real reasons behind those feelings are critical skills for connecting to your true core beliefs about you.*

By the way, how many different feeling words do you think there are in the English language? Most people believe that there must be thousands. This is true. You will need a way to organize your thinking about feelings, for the purpose of building a feeling vocabulary, and for helping you to learn to identify and understand what you are feeling.

All feelings experienced by humans can be divided into five broad categories: happy, sad, angry, afraid, and confused. All feelings words will fit in *one or more* of these categories. Using one full sheet of paper for each category, see how many feelings you can list in each category. At first you may have difficulty identifying feelings in one or more of the categories. Do not become discouraged. This is your Primitive-Self's latest attempt to make you give up and accept failure. Make a conscious decision to see the exercise as a challenge to have fun with, instead of something negative. In approaching it this way, you are keeping your healthy Meta-Self in control of your thinking and behavior. Spend some time every day building the vocabulary lists and learning to recognize and actually feel your feelings.

By the way, some feelings will fit in more than one category. These are feelings that are general or vague in nature. The more specific a feeling is, the more you will see that it fits only one category. (See Appendix A for a sample of feeling words.)

Uncovering your true core beliefs is the ultimate goal for learning to identify and really feel your feelings. In working to accomplish this goal, your next task is to attach reasons to each of the feelings that you discover about you. As you collect your feelings, identify the reason or reasons for each of them. Use the following sentence map to write them down in your journal. In your journal writing, expand on your "feeling and reason" statements to explore and discover your true beliefs about yourself.

Complete the sentence map for each feeling experienced. Be sure to feel the emotion.

"I feel_____because_____."

Here are two examples:

"I feel sad because I realize that my mother was never emotionally there for me."

"I feel relieved because I have an idea what's wrong in my mind and I see how I can change it."

The model for the sentence map was adapted from Robert R Carkhuff's *The Art of Helping* (Human Resources Development Press, 1980).

Journaling to You about You

If you are not writing, you are not growing.

Learning to write to yourself about yourself is a critical part of the self-change process. Writing your thoughts and feelings in black and white makes you pay attention to your thinking and take responsibility for your thoughts. Journaling will be difficult at first because your Primitive-Self will resist your attempts to know its true thinking. You may not like to write, or you may believe you are a poor writer. You may feel that you are too busy to devote time to it. You might think it's silly or that you do better just thinking about yourself. These reasons (excuses) are all resistance to you discovering the truth about you. They are resistance to discovery and real change, and they originate in your Primitive-Self. Overrule them. Get to work. Hold yourself accountable for doing the work necessary to increasing the quality of your life. If you give in to your Primitive-Self and stop writing, you will not be growing.

Journaling to you about you should be scheduled for *at least* three times per week, for a minimum of one hour for each session. Remember, the more often you work at it, the faster change will happen. In the beginning you must schedule appointments with yourself for writing. Schedule it in writing, on a calendar or in your Day-Timer. Do not rely on your memory—your Primitive-Self will make you procrastinate or forget. Keeping your commitment to yourself to write is an important way to learn to constructively hold yourself accountable for constructive behavior. Do not minimize its importance—that is your Primitive-Self leading you once again to failure.

Save every journal entry. Be sure to put them in a safe, private place; they are for your eyes only, unless you elect to share them. My patients share them with me as part of the therapeutic process. Sharing them holds you accountable for doing the work in the beginning of the process of change; your resistance is strongest at the beginning. If you do share your writing, be careful with whom you share. A competent helper is one who is objective and knows more than you do about being healthy. Choose wisely—all "help" is not helpful. You may have to find a professional helper to give you more objective, constructive feedback. In any case, save your writing. It is a record of your progress that can be used later to facilitate further change. Saving your journaling also gives you a way to look back and see how much you have changed. After a few months of consistent effort, you will be amazed at the change you have accomplished.

During the journaling sessions, expect resistance to completing the task. "I can't think of anything to write." "I really need to be washing the clothes." "I've got things I really need to be doing for work." "The kids need my attention now—I can do this later." "I'm just too confused right now, and I'm not feeling anything." These reasons are all resistance by your Primitive-Self to you achieving your goals of connecting with your real self and seeing the truth. Remember, your old self, your Primitive-Self, does not want to be seen or to change. It is comfortable with its present state, regardless of its (your) unhappiness or disfunctionality. Challenge and work through its resistance to you having a happier and fulfilling life.

In your work building a vocabulary of feeling words, you will probably notice that there are words in the same category with similar meanings but of different intensity. For example, annoyed, peeved, mad, furious, and infuriated are all in the Anger category but the intensity increases across the list. Accurately responding to yourself and others requires the appropriate intensity of feeling.

Following are some examples of initial journal entries.

Example 1: Ted's Journal Entry, (Week 2)

Honestly, I'm confused about what you want me to write. I think this is what you want. This is me talking to myself. You have to stop thinking that you are not good enough, and you have to start being more confident in the person you are. You have to take control of your life and cherish what is important to you, like your family and friends. All this other stuff is holding you back from who you really are. You know you are a very caring person, and you needed to stop being afraid of showing that side of yourself to others. You have to start believing in yourself and stop doubting yourself all the time. When problems arise, you have to hit them head on and not let them build to be more than they are by not addressing them. You have to take control of your life. You have to stop dwelling on your mistakes in the past.

Ted is attempting to follow my instructions to talk to himself about himself. Instead, he is lecturing himself in a very critical manner. It has the tone or feel of a parent scolding a child. However, his writing does reveal some important information about what he believes to be true about his self. He just cannot see it yet. At this early point of the change process, Ted cannot hear what he is really saying.

Journal Dialogue	What Ted Is Really Saying
"You are not good enough"	(I am an inferior person)
"Start being more confident"	(I lack self-confidence) or (I am incompetent)
"You have to take control of your life"	(I have lost control of my life)

Journal Dialogue	What Ted Is Really Saying
"Stop being afraid of showing that you care for others"	(I am afraid to risk being hurt)
"Start believing in yourself"	(I have lost faith in myself)
"Stop doubting yourself"	(I don't trust my mind to tell me the truth)

What Ted is really saying about himself is different from what he actually writes. To an objective observer, Ted's writing is a reflection of his early learned primitive beliefs. In his Primitive-Self, he is attacking himself the same way his parents did when he was a young child. Psychologically, Ted is still a child and his own critical parent. He owns his known (believed) deficits, but he does nothing to consider their validity or to correct them. They are just part of who he is. If Ted had been able to develop a Meta-Self, he would have the ability to constructively evaluate and correct any real deficits. He would also know how to discount any beliefs that are irrational.

Example 2: Sara's Journal Entry, (Week 3)

Sara, for most of your life you have struggled with feelings of loneliness, shame, and of being inferior to others. Think about your loneliness. Go back as far as you can remember—maybe four or five years old. You were alone quite often, or even when your parents were near, you remember being lonely. You played alone; you walked through fields and woods alone. One of your companions was a cow. You would taunt the cow and try to get it to chase you. You spent long days playing alone in the creek near the house. Where was your mom? Did she wonder where you were? Could she see you from the house? She always seemed sad, and numb, like she was always lost in her own thoughts. Sara, you didn't really like being alone, but you had no choice.

Your mom didn't seem to like you much, so you stayed out of her way, unless your dad was home. Mom would talk when Dad was around. Mom always seemed to be very quiet or very angry. She would yank you by the arms, and holding your little body up, she would hit you anywhere— she was so angry. Why doesn't she love me? What did I do? Just behave, stop making her angry, and don't you get angry, because you'll just make a fool of yourself, and she will feel worse. Just go away, don't be seen, be quiet. Sara, you are an ungrateful little shit.

Sara is recounting her early childhood in an attempt to accept the reality of it. Sara talks to herself in the second person, as is she *is* another person. She is not yet really feeling her feelings. She is struggling to get through the wall that blocks her ability to feel. In the process she triggers and reverts to her Primitive-Self and begins talking in the first person about herself. In her Primitive-Self she can feel her fear, loneliness, and desperation just as she did at six years old. Sara has connected with the real feelings and thoughts of her Primitive-Self. Her next step will be to connect a sufficient amount of primitive thoughts, feelings, and reasons to identify her core beliefs.

Identifying Core Beliefs

You must know your core beliefs
before you can change them.

The goal of this exercise is to help you learn to identify and understand the nature of core beliefs. As you read about these people's lives and begin to understand about core beliefs, be sure to watch for beliefs that apply to you. List them in your journal, and write about them in detail.

Example 1: Katie's Core Beliefs, (Week 5)

Refer back to chapter 2, page (6), and the story of Katie. Through the hard work of reconnecting to her real self, Katie discovered her core beliefs:

"I have little faith in my value as a person"

"I am unlovable"

"I am a failure in relationships"

"I don't have faith in me"

Katie's experience as a child was one of *psychological* neglect and abuse. She did not go hungry, and she was not beaten. Her scars are not physical ones. They are in her mind, residing there as crippling beliefs about herself. Katie was taught by both of her parents that she had little or no value as a person. Katie's opinions, needs, and desires were at best ignored. She was left to herself and lived in fear of her father. She felt hurt and abandoned by her family. Katie learned to believe that she was unlovable. She also learned that to trust anyone would lead to more hurt. Katie's only option was to isolate physically and mentally from everyone—especially her real self.

The reasons for Katie's negative core beliefs were not immediately evident to her, but through a determined effort on her part and the help of a good professional helper, she was able to identify and understand the reasons for her adopting these negative beliefs and begin to understand their destructive power over her life. Now that she knows her real enemy—her own early learned beliefs—she can begin to change her life for the better.

Example 2: Ted's Self-Discovery, (Week 6)

I have decided that I am very weak in the self-esteem area. I lack self-confidence and self-respect. I doubt myself all the time. I find myself thinking about my dad a lot—how he always told me I wouldn't amount to much. I tell myself it doesn't matter, but I guess it really does. I think I can see where some of this feeling of worthlessness comes from. It controls my life. I have always told myself that I'm just a shy person, but I see now that I am really just scared to death. I always feel judged by others—like they are always looking down on me. Deep down I know it's just my own insecurity. No one has ever believed in me. Maybe I just need to figure out how to just love myself and even like me.

Progress can be observed in Ted's writing. He is speaking in the first person now and identifying and owning his feelings. He has also opened up to deeper thoughts and memories and is looking for reasons from the past that make him feel so bad about himself. He is kinder to himself and more objective, instead of being emotionally irrational. He is beginning to make sense. He is beginning to think with reasoning. He is making progress in learning to be his own self-advocate. *He is beginning to experience and live in his Meta-Self.*

What do you think are Ted's core beliefs about himself? Use the information about Ted in this chapter plus Ted's journal and analysis in chapter 2. How many of Ted's core beliefs match your own?

Identifying Core Beliefs of Your Primitive-Self

Now it's time for you to focus on identifying your own core beliefs. Your goal is to identify the core beliefs of your Primitive-Self that are limiting or impeding your growth and fulfillment. Once they are identified, you will know which beliefs you want to keep and those that need to be replaced by new, healthier beliefs. Discovering your core beliefs is not easy to accomplish, but it is imperative that you work at it until you know them all. Reading books, journal writing, and observing your thoughts and behavior are the primary means to learn what your real self believes.

Reading

There are many books available that can help you connect with your real self. I have provided you with a starter list of books in Appendix B. As you read, you must emotionally connect with what the author is saying in order to profit from reading. Just reading the words or not paying attention to what you are reading will not work. Get involved by feeling. Search for truth about you in what you read.

Writing

Write an autobiography. Writing the story of your life can be an eye-opening experience. Be sure to include your earliest memories and any recurring dreams. Try to discern what they say about you as a person. If you cannot remember back as far as the age of five, find something or someone to jog your memory. Old pictures and conversations with family members and old friends may help you remember. Be sure to include in your story any important people in your life, especially romantic relationships. Keep in mind that you learn more about yourself from failures than you do from successes.

Behavior Observation

Every day, observe your thoughts, feelings, and behavior for indicators of deeper beliefs about yourself and the world.

- » Identify each feeling and reason experienced.
- » Identify the facet of self that is in control: Primitive-Self, Surface-Self, or Meta-Self.
- » If it is not the Meta-Self, then move your thinking to the Meta-Self perspective and reevaluate your thinking.
- » Create healthy responses from your Meta-Self (for example, how you would prefer to have been parented).

Remember, your goal is to know your true core beliefs about you and assess their validity from the perspective of your Meta-Self. Once you have identified your negative, irrational, and destructive beliefs, you will be capable of replacing them with healthful, beneficial beliefs.

Observing and Responding to Feelings and Reasons Observed in Others

Internally you are learning to connect to the real you. Connecting with the real you is essential to learning how to nourish your real self. Later, you will learn to relate to others with your real self so that you can achieve being nourished by them. As part of the learning process you must also learn how to nourish others. In order to nourish others, you must *have and communicate empathy*. Learning to be empathetic begins with knowing and understanding yourself. The healthier you become, the more ability and energy you will have to give to others.

Learning to be in contact with your own feelings and thinking can be enhanced by focusing on feelings and reasons observed in others. A word of caution is in order. When you first begin, identifying the feelings and reasons experienced in others is often more difficult than identifying your own. You must be able to put aside your frame of reference—your perception of how you would feel and why you would feel that way. Instead you must connect with the other person's perception of their experience. As you gain competence in this internal form of empathy for others, you will be able to better understand others and communicate that understanding.

Watch others when they are not speaking, and guess what they are feeling. At this stage of your learning, there is no risk of being embarrassed about being wrong, because you don't have to ask the person if your guess is correct. If they are speaking, listen for their verbal expressions of their feelings. If they do not say a feeling, listen to their voice tone, inflection, facial expressions, and the content of their words to identify feelings. After you identify a feeling you think they are experiencing, think of the reason—*from their perception of their experience*—that is causing them to feel it. Remember, to be accurate, your responses to the person must be from their frame of reference (perception). Your response to them is about their experience, not yours. It is not about how *you would feel* or for the reason you think they *should* have for a particular feeling.

After you have practiced guessing for a few days, be brave—risk actually responding to someone, and ask the other person if you are accurate. Remember, like any skill, identifying feelings and reasons in yourself and others is learned only through focused practice. Be patient and persistent in your efforts. A word of caution: you will only be successful at responding to others to the extent you have opened up to your own real feelings about yourself and their reasons.

After you have had sufficient practice in silently identifying feelings and reasons expressed by others, you will be ready to respond out loud in conversations. Don't let fear stop you; remember you are supposed to be challenging your fears. In my experience, people are a lot better at responding than they initially think they will be. Work to make your responses short, clear, and accurate. Be sure to give the other person time to respond. Watch for the person's verbal or nonverbal recognition that you are accurate. You may be surprised how well you do.

Sentence Map for Actual Responding

You feel_____because_____.

In Summary

People generally believe that they know their real selves. In reality, most are only aware of a portion of their real psychological selves, and the more psychologically troubled or impaired a person is, the less he is consciously connected to his real self.

In fact, most people remain unaware of the deepest beliefs that drive their thought processes and ultimately all of their behavior. In order to increase the psychological quality of your life, you must uncover and evaluate the quality of your deepest core beliefs. Then you must take responsibility for changing any belief or behavior that impedes your mental health, psychological growth, and fulfillment.

It has been my experience that most negative core beliefs people hold prove to be either irrational or untrue. But neither my professional opinion nor the opinion of anyone else means anything to a person who has lived with negative core beliefs for a lifetime. To him, they are his reality; they are all he knows. An individual's negative beliefs, especially about his self, override all outside opinions. *Only the individual has the power to know and change his core beliefs. It is by conscious choice that an individual must begin this process of learning to identify and change his harmful, self-destructive beliefs.*

Individuals that have engaged their Meta Selves demonstrate more objective and responsible thinking in similar ways: "My way of making sense of the world and getting what I want and need is not working. My attempts to solve my problems do not work." " I must accept that at least part, if not all, of my problems are because of me—who I am and who I am not." "I must find out what is wrong with me."

Producing real and constructive change in your life begins with connecting with and owning the real you. What are the core beliefs that determine the quality and content of everything you think and do? These are the beliefs that determine the value you place on you, as a person, and what you see as possible for you in life. Discovering what you really believe as truth about you is essential, because you cannot change what you do not know.

In this chapter you have observed people who have struggled with the process of getting in touch with their real selves and their true beliefs. By this point in your reading, I trust that you have opened your mind to identify with these people and have begun to connect with your real self. A word of caution is in order. Establishing a conscious connection with your real self is just the beginning of the process of change. It is the first major step in engaging and building your healthy self—your Meta-Self. Your Meta-Self is the facet of your mind that maintains this conscious connection and guides your growth to a fulfilling future.

Your next challenge will be to assess the validity and functionality of your beliefs that guide your every thought, feeling, and action. Your goal is to construct a rational, healthy, adult self, a Meta-Self that is built on functional reality and reasoned thinking. As you begin to build a functional new self, you will begin to experience the self-satisfaction and fulfillment that grows out of a positive, rational, and reality-based belief structure.

Stay determined and focused on constructive self change; you have much more to learn and much more to accomplish to get to where you need and want to be.

If you are not consistently journaling, you are not growing. You have temporarily regressed to being controlled by your Primitive-Self. Psychological growth is always two steps forward of progress and one step backward of regression to old behaviors. Get back into your Meta-Self, and hold yourself accountable. Schedule regular, prioritized appointments with yourself to read and write. You must learn to live in your healthy Meta-Self—all the time.

6

Conscious Development of Your Meta-Self

In the psychological domain, you learn by experiencing. You must live in your Meta-Self to understand its benefits and increase its power to govern your life.

What You Have Learned So Far

Chapter 1 presented the concept of "self," its elements, and the importance of having a positive and rational self-concept. You were introduced to the facets of the self: the Primitive-Self, the Surface-Self, and the Meta-Self. You learned about the process of healthy self-development and the power of early learned beliefs in the formation of self-concept. A reality-based and positive sense of self is the essential basis for healthy psychological development and the ability to sustain mental health throughout one's lifetime. On the other hand, having a negative self-concept will lead to a life of emotional deficits, interpersonal problems, and psychological deterioration over the course of a lifetime.

You were introduced to the developmental causes and the emotional and behavioral indicators of a troubled and divided self: not having faith in yourself, not trusting your mind to know truth, having fear as your primary motivator, not trusting others to know the real you, having experienced life as a series of personal disappointments, and feeling discouraged about who you have become.

You learned that the course and quality of your life can be greatly improved if you are willing to identify and own the real problem. You learned that real change in the quality of your life requires learning the truth about the erroneous and harmful beliefs that you hold as truth about yourself, and changing them to positive, valid, and constructive beliefs.

Chapter 2 presented the characteristics of a divided, troubled self and the problem of your own natural resistance to change of any kind, even beneficial change. You learned that once early learned beliefs are accepted as truth, and regardless of their false or harmful nature, it is difficult for a person to change them. This is especially true if the beliefs are about who you are as a person. You also learned that if your beliefs about you are positive and beneficial, they form the basis for normal, healthy psychological development and emotional fulfillment in life. If your beliefs about you are negative and harmful, they will be a huge obstacle to overcome. As an example, if you learned, as a child, to believe that you are unlovable and therefore have less value than others, you are sure to carry this irrational and destructive belief into adulthood, with potentially disastrous results.

Chapter 3 examined the role your mind plays in establishing and maintaining mental health. Depending on the quality of its content and thought processes, your mind either works for you as your ally or against you as your enemy. Also presented was a discussion about the meaning and role of identifying and living constructive truth, both objective and subjective, and a look at its practical application to self-development. Next, the chapter focused on the critical role reasoning plays in psychological development and the sustaining of mental health throughout life. Particular emphasis was placed on the effective blending of reason and emotion. Finally a comparison between reasoned and unreasoned thinking was presented.

Chapter 4 presented the concept of the Meta-Self as the healthy facet of your mind that is able to be objective and can learn and employ reasoned thinking to identify functional truth. You learned that an underdeveloped Meta-Self is the result of an early life experience of being dominated by a negative Primitive-Self, which has kept you from growing psychologically. You learned that to make real constructive change happen, you have to identify the true nature and content of your Primitive-Self, and that you must identify, reject, and replace the limiting and destructive negative beliefs you have held as truth. These negative and self-limiting beliefs must be replaced with a new, constructive, beneficial set of beliefs. You learned that constructive Meta-Self beliefs will include rational, productive principles that will enable you to live a more positive and fulfilling life. In addition, the chapter explored the critical role the Meta-Self plays in consciously directing positive change and establishing its own position as the exclusive manager of your mind.

Chapter 5 introduced the initial steps in the process of change, in the form of cognitive and behavioral exercises. These exercises are designed to enable you to get in touch with your real self and to help you learn to constructively manage the quality of your thinking. You learned that getting in touch with who you really are—what you really believe as the truth about you—is the first important goal in making real change take place. Knowing what you really believe to be the truth about you is critical to positive change, because you cannot replace a detrimental belief if you remain unaware of its existence.

You were also cautioned that the ability to connect with your real self may prove to be a challenge because of your Primitive-Self's resistance to being known. You must learn to identify this resistance from the perspective of your Meta-Self and rebound from the regressive episodes that *will* occur. You learned that to be successful, to make real and lasting change happen, the exercises must be repeated many times before consistent and lasting success can be realized. The actual number of repetitions depends on the degree of separation you have from your real self, the amount of resistance to change you generate, and the amount of effort you put into achieving results. Remember, your Primitive-Self is going to resist doing the work to change. One indicator to watch for—a *red flag* that warns you that your Primitive-Self is taking control—is that you have stopped journaling. Writing down your feelings and reasons helps you to own your real self and take responsibility for how well it is operating. It activates your Meta-Self. Another common indicator of resistance is procrastination: finding seemingly valid reasons to put off reading, writing, and risking new behaviors.

By this point in your learning process, you have probably experienced both success and failure in your attempts to understand and incorporate what has been presented. This is to be expected. Remember, you are attempting to change negative beliefs and behaviors that have been a part of who you are for as long as you can recall. Some, if not many, of your deepest beliefs have been unknown to you until recently, and you have gotten used to living without knowing or wanting to know that they exist. Your Primitive-Self was intent on hiding their content from your awareness. Your Primitive-Self is not going to cooperate with any attempt to change just because you are aware of your negative beliefs.

Overcoming your own resistance to knowing your own true beliefs about yourself is probably the hardest thing you have attempted in your life. Be patient with yourself. Be positive about yourself. Be persistent with your desire and efforts to discover the truth, and remain steadfast in your goal of increasing the quality of your life. *Being patient, positive, and persistent with yourself are important elements of your new self—your Meta-Self.*

The Meta-Self: Establishing Healthy Beliefs as Principles for Living

Universal meta-value number three is about pursuing self-development in all domains of life, throughout life—especially the psychological domain. Living healthfully requires fostering and maintaining a lifestyle of responsible psychological growth. The bottom line is that you, the individual, have a choice. Are you going to grow psychologically as you pass through life, or are you going to deteriorate psychologically? Regardless of your present level of psychological health and functioning, you will not stay at that level. As a human being, you cannot avoid the fact that you will experience the challenges life presents and the personal changes they produce. It is inevitable that everyone will change throughout life, because we all face known and unknown experiences of all types and complexity. Your beliefs about you and life will determine your effectiveness in dealing with what life presents. You will either meet those challenges successfully, or you will fail to some degree. Either way, you will change, for better or worse.

As you have discovered in starting the process of changing yourself for the better, the work is not easy, nor is it a rapid process. It takes determination, patience, and the ability to incorporate new learning as part of you to make real constructive change happen. To sustain constructive change over a lifetime, you need commitment to its value and you need direction about building your Meta-Self.

Building Your Meta-Self

Two steps forward, one backward.

If you have been successful in beginning the process of changing yourself for the better, you have experienced some success in distinguishing the three facets of your self. Your final goal is to live full-time in your Meta-Self and to consciously manage your Primitive and Surface selves. However, as you probably have discovered by this point in your efforts, it is not easy to stay in your Meta-Self. Your Primitive-Self is always trying to reassert its power. When it is successful, this is known as regression or sliding back into your Primitive-Self. Unfortunately, regression is *always* a part of the change process. Psychological change for the better is always a process of two steps forward and one backward. Be patient with yourself, accept your failures, and redouble your effort to grow and hold on to the growth once it is achieved.

As you have probably experienced, the more you can keep your Meta-Self in control of your thinking, the better you feel about yourself. However, building the new knowledge and power necessary to sustain your Meta-Self is a process of trial and error. At first it will be difficult to hold on to the Meta-Self perspective, because your Primitive-Self is so dominant. It will take time and persistent effort to increase your Meta-Self's power. As you develop the power of your Meta-Self, you will be able to keep it in control for longer and longer periods of time. Requiring yourself to stay in your Meta-Self builds its power and diminishes your Primitive-Self's power. Don't wait for an emotional problem or crisis to think about "using" your Meta-Self. Remember, your goal must be to *live* in your Meta-Self. Building its staying power in unemotional times is essential, because the more emotional you become, the more difficult it is to assume the Meta-Self perspective, or to stay in it if you were already there.

By this time you should have uncovered some surprising and disturbing beliefs that you hold about yourself. You are also recognizing the limiting and destructive effects of these negative beliefs on your ability to experience psychological health and quality. These beliefs may seem overwhelming, but *they are just beliefs, beliefs that you can change*. Remember, your decision to develop a healthy, adult Meta-Self is just that—a decision. It is a decision to create a more healthful and rewarding life. It is a decision to choose personal responsibility and courage as the primary motivators for all thoughts and actions. It is a decision to be consciously connected to all facets of one's real self and to develop that self to its fullest capacity and maturity.

This chapter is about how to further build, strengthen, and refine your Meta-Self. Developing your Meta-Self is accomplished by first establishing a conscious connection with your real self from the perspective of your Meta-Self, and then by constructing a real self that is positive, self-nourishing, and nourishing to others. It is about constructing a rational, mature, and psychologically healthful set of principles about yourself, your behavior, and your perceptions of the outside world. As you achieve success in learning how to govern your life from the perspective of a Meta-Self, you will experience an improved and positive perception of yourself. You will begin to build faith in yourself, and your empowered Meta-Self will effectively guide your continued growth and change as you continue to refine its content and manage its processes.

Reasoning versus Childhood and Cultural Beliefs

*Everything you believe is fair game for
rational reevaluation.*

Choosing to live a life directed by a healthy Meta-Self requires that one pursues and lives truth and reality. Achieving this goal requires an open-minded approach to accurate knowledge about yourself and the world. This can only be achieved through reasoned thinking.

As you seek to build principles to guide your life in a healthy direction, be aware that your current beliefs were shaped by your family of origin and also the culture in which you live. Because most of this learning occurred early in your life, it can easily be taken for granted as being truth and therefore remain unchallenged. Were all of the beliefs you learned as a child valid? If some were valid then, are they still valid? Remember, everything you do is driven by your beliefs, whether you are aware of them or not. In order to be mentally healthy, everything you learned to believe is fair game for rational reevaluation. Be open to evaluating everything for rationality, beneficial truth, and functionality.

Some of the cultural beliefs you have learned are valid—if they are beneficial and actually lived. You have the responsibility to choose wisely, from your culture and others, the beliefs that stand up to reasoned thinking. It is also your responsibility to reject any beliefs that reasoned thinking cannot support.

For example, you should not accept anything as truth just because a majority of people see it as so. To be mentally sound is to believe that reasoning rules, not numbers. Consider any belief you learned in childhood that is held by most people. As children, we are taught that if most people believe something to be true, then it must be true—right? No! The number or status of the believers has no relevance to truth. The fact that millions of people believe something does not make it valid, rational, or beneficial. Any belief, from any source, must be evaluated through your own reasoned thinking. *There are no exceptions.* If you insist on making exceptions, you will be undermining your own thinking and limiting your psychological growth. You cannot retain the early learned belief that says, "It is okay to be aware that two ideas contradict each other and just let them coexist as truth." If you agree with this, belief you are, in effect, saying ...

» I am just not smart enough to decide what is true,

» I don't have the right to ask for or demand truth, and

>   » I relinquish the power to decide truth to others.

You may have already observed that much of what you learned as truth in your youth was faulty. As an adult, it is your responsibility to evaluate what you have been taught and change the beliefs that do not hold up to reality, especially those that have been harmful to your well-being. I have already discussed what parents unknowingly teach their children to believe about themselves and how false and destructive those beliefs can be. But also consider the validity of what they taught you as truth about other things. It is your responsibility to evaluate all you have been taught about everything and replace the invalid, irrational, and harmful beliefs with something better. If you do not, you will repeat many of the mistakes of your parents.

Challenging early learned or popularly held beliefs will often lead to criticism from those who do not agree. Learn to support your views through reasoned thinking prior to your attempts to express your views to others. When others disagree, attempt a rational discussion, but be prepared to find that others who do not reason well or are not open-minded will be unable or unwilling to see anything in a new way. During these disagreements and even afterward, be careful of prolonged periods of doubting yourself. You may be slipping into your Primitive-Self. Review your thinking repeatedly to be sure of your reasoning. The more you practice expressing your views from the perspective of your Meta-Self, the more your confidence will grow.

Universal Meta-Self Principles

The development of your Meta-Self begins with adopting and living the three universal meta-principles that are fundamental to all other psychological principles and values that are beneficial (see chapter 5 for a review):

>   » To know, value, and live in functional reality—truth

» To know, value, and live conscious, constructive, reasoned thinking

» To know, value, and live a lifestyle of psychological growth

Other Suggested Meta-Self Principles—A Starter List

In addition to the universal meta-principles, and as a product of them, you must build an extensive *conscious* set of constructive, beneficial life principles. Building your Meta-Self is predicated on building these personal principles as values that you actually live. The following are examples of beliefs that could be adopted as principles for incorporation into your life. Use it as a beginning point for building your own personal set of principles.

Examples of Meta-Self Principles

I am physically, intellectually, and emotionally responsible for me.

I am competent in relating with others.

I relate with empathy, respect, and understanding.

I live with courage as my primary motivator and view taking risks for growth as positive.

I am responsible for deciding functional truth in every case, and then for living it.

I am my own self-advocate. I believe in me.

I hold myself accountable for doing what is positive and productive in every part of my life.

I seek ways to be productive and achieve—achievement allows me to feel good about me.

I identify anything I fear and challenge it.

In relationships I give to others what I expect, need, or want from them.

I stay in my Meta-Self and exercise it daily to grow and maintain its power.

*Your new, constructive Meta-Self principles
must be lived to be real.*

Remember, it will do you no good to only write down principles and then return to thinking and behaving as you have done in the past. These new, constructive Meta-Self principles must be lived consciously at all times, and you must hold yourself accountable for living them. In addition, you must be ready to revise and refine your principles by observing and evaluating your experience of them as you apply them in your everyday life. They must be continuously evaluated for validity, appropriate application, congruence, and functionality. Also, you need to watch your daily life and search your experience for more new, healthy principles to add to your list. You will discover how all constructive principles are interrelated and interdependent. The more you work on developing your new Meta-Self, the more sense it will make to you. And you will know you are on the right path, because you will feel consistently better about who you are.

I must emphasize that your Meta-Self—your healthy, adult self—will not develop without *constant, conscious* effort. As an analogy consider muscle development in the physical domain of life. A person can read about building larger, stronger muscles; he can watch videos of workouts; and he can think about his desire to bulk up. None of these activities will build muscles. The only way to actually build muscles is to use them, to actually work them. The same is true in building your Meta-Self. Make a constant, committed effort to distinguish the difference in the thinking processes and content of your Primitive-Self and your Meta-Self. As stated earlier, your goal must be to hold yourself accountable for staying in your Meta-Self. You will find it hard at first to determine which self is in control of your thinking. Keep working to learn from your mistakes—your slips back to your Primitive-Self. Your best indication that you have slipped is the presence of negative feelings or no feelings at all. The best indicator of being in your Meta-Self is that your thinking is positive, rational, and beneficial. At the feeling level, your Meta-Self is always aware of your feelings, but it prioritizes knowing the reasons for any particular feeling, knowing the validity of those reasons, and deciding what constructive action should be taken. You must also hold yourself accountable for consistently behaving in new ways dictated by your Meta-Self. It is not enough just to think more responsibly and healthfully; you must live healthful truth.

Constructing Meta-Self Principles

Building your meta-principles is a conscious, ordered process that seeks to incorporate and integrate relevant facts that respect reality and identify functional, subjective truth. These truths become the foundation of the new principles you adopt and live.

From the perspective of your Meta-Self, learn to hold yourself accountable for ...

» Objectively observing your thoughts, feelings, and actions. Compile truth about you. Substantiate things you value. Own deficits in your thinking and behavior. Develop programs to change those things that are harmful to you.

» Evaluating thoughts, feelings, and actions for origin (cause), validity, and how and when to appropriately express them.

» Building a library of opinions and concepts you believe in because you have used reasoned thinking to formulate them as truth.

» Valuing functional, beneficial truth over myth, previous learning, tradition, the status quo, and the opinion of authorities.

» Evaluating all beliefs for congruence (noncontradiction). Watch for exceptions to perceived truth. Any given truth may not apply in all cases. Develop justifiable concepts to support your position about these exceptions.

You must learn to parent your Primitive-Self.

Your Meta-Self's Role as Parent to Your Primitive-Self

As a troubled adult with a mind dominated by a destructive Primitive-Self, you live a divided life. You try to act like an adult, but you feel like a child. Your Primitive-Self still desires acceptance, love, approval, and validation from parents who never gave it to you. Your Primitive-Self still hopes they can be who they never were.

By now your developing Meta-Self knows that your parents will never be able to give you what they don't have. You must find another way to nourish yourself. The answer lies once again in the development of your Meta-Self. You must learn to parent yourself.

The experience of having primitive thoughts and feelings and having them responded to in an appropriate manner is what your parents were supposed to provide when you were a child. Now that you are learning to live in your Meta-Self, it is your responsibility to care for and manage your Primitive-Self—to parent it. It is your Meta-Self's task to supervise your primitive, negative thinking and its attempts to behave in any dysfunctional or destructive manner. The more you develop the power of your Meta-Self, the better you will be able to perform these parenting tasks. With time and persistence, you will become your own nourishing parent.

As I stated earlier, the failure of one's Meta-Self to develop because of the dominance of a negative Primitive-Self originates in early childhood. As life precedes to adulthood, the child with a negative sense of self—a troubled, divided self—may continue to develop physically and intellectually. However, because of the dominance of a negative Primitive-Self, growth of the psychological self is greatly restricted, if not completely halted. An abused or neglected child is stuck in a reality where the attributes that form and strengthen a Meta-Self cannot develop. Without the development of attributes such as a positive sense of self and the ability to reason, the child has no way to intercede and redirect the Primitive-Self. As the troubled child proceeds through the preteen and teen years, he becomes more and more separated from the reality of his negative self. Growing to chronological adulthood and facing the challenges presented by adult life compounds the problem.

Although a major goal of this process is to stay in your Meta-Self for longer and longer periods, it is important that you keep a conscious connection with your Primitive-Self, even though it is diminishing in power. From the perspective of your Meta-Self, learn as much about your Primitive-Self's thinking processes and beliefs as you can. Keeping a conscious connection is the only way to gain and keep control of its negative influence.

To accomplish this task, you must be open to any negative feelings originating in your Primitive-Self. Negative feelings are the doorway to the negative thoughts (beliefs) of your Primitive-Self. Remember, your feelings are caused by your thoughts. Once you identify a negative feeling and the reason or reasons that precede it, write it down. Then, from your Meta-Self's view, take time to see and evaluate your Primitive-Self's perception, and write them both in your journal. Writing your thoughts and feelings from the different facets of your self makes you pay concrete attention to them and take responsibility for their content. Always end this learning experience by thinking and acting on the event from the perspective of your Meta-Self.

Cognitive Exercise for Your Meta-Self

The ability of your Meta-Self to think with reasoning is a learned skill that must be practiced until it becomes part of you. Expressing your reasoned views to others was discussed previously as an effective means of gaining proficiency and confidence. Obviously, as a prerequisite to risking your reasoned thinking with others, you should first achieve some internal proficiency at reasoned thinking. You can use any current issue or recall anything from history and construct arguments to support your opinions. You may also use your own personal history to develop your skill and confidence.

For example, recall instances from your childhood when you disagreed with your peers, parents, or other adults, where you thought you were right but could not get the other person to see your view or maybe even listen. Examine those instances for the quality of your thinking as well as that of the other person. Is there a better way you could have viewed the incident or expressed yourself? Maybe you did an adequate job, but it just fell on deaf ears. What were the holes in each party's position? Perhaps neither of you was dealing with the real issue. Construct a new argument if you believe you were right. If you were wrong, own it, and review the reasoning that supports your new position.

Remember, you must learn to value truth over anything else, and your only method of discovering it is reasoned thinking, implemented and guided by your Meta-Self.

Learning from Regressive Episodes

At this point in the process of change, you have learned more about how to distinguish between your Primitive, Surface, and Meta selves. You have accomplished this by engaging and learning to observe your thinking and behavior from the perspective of your Meta-Self. However, you are probably still confused at times about which one is in control of your thinking. Early in the change process, the best way to distinguish Meta-Self thinking from Primitive-Self thinking is that Meta-Self thinking includes positive action to challenge or solve your negative experience. *A Primitive-Self only focuses on safety, suffering, or escaping.*

Remember, learning to live with your Meta-Self in control is a mentally challenging process that will require both consistent determination and patience. You are going to experience periods when your Meta-Self loses control and your Primitive-Self takes over. This transfer of power can happen without your immediate awareness—for example, "I don't need to think about it. I just know I'm right." This is a red flag; you need to think (reason) about everything. When these episodes occur, catch yourself as soon as possible and consciously change back to your Meta-Self perspective. With determined practice you will learn to minimize the degree and length of your regressive episodes, and even to stop them all together. Remember, learning to identify and stop these regressive episodes successfully depends upon being aware, at all times, of which facet of your self is in control of your thought processes. Observe the quality of your thinking about everything from your Meta-Self perspective.

Be advised that your Primitive-Self is not going to relinquish control of your mind easily, because it is fighting for its dominance over your thought processes as well as its own perceived existence. You are especially vulnerable to regression any time when stress is high and feelings are more intense than usual. During these times, slow down your thinking, get control, and then single out a feeling and its reason. Stay in or get into your Meta-Self. Don't let yourself be swept into a whirlwind of negative thoughts and emotions.

There are several ways that the Primitive-Self reasserts its power. Its triggers are important to know. Emotional stress is a primary trigger. Increased pressure at work, a relationship problem, and unexpected expense are all causes of emotional stress. The Primitive-Self can also induce confused thinking, negative thinking, negative feelings, cutting off from feelings, or a general mental fogginess, and it can create illogical thinking that seems logical on the surface. These are just a few of the ways the Primitive-Self reasserts its power.

One way to identify which facet of your self is in control is to observe the outcomes of thoughts and feelings. If negative thinking leads to more negative thoughts and feelings, this is a phenomenon known as a "negative spiral." It is a common feature of destructive, primitive thinking.

On the other hand, Meta-Self thinking is productive. You may experience negative or self-critical thinking in the normal course of living, but it will be followed by productive internal exploration, understanding, and constructive resolution. With the Meta-Self in charge, constructive thinking and action are always present. Problems are not ignored or denied; they are solved in healthful, beneficial ways.

A healthy mind does not wallow in misery. It is not excessively self-critical. It does not remain in a state of confused thinking. It does not accept failure. It knows or finds constructive truth. Your Meta-Self will work to find a workable solution that allows you to feel good about yourself for having confronted the problem constructively. The Primitive-Self recycles self-criticism and negative thinking and feeling to the point of exhaustion and emotional numbness. It does not solve anything. You are always left feeling bad about yourself or not feeling at all.

Another indication that your Primitive-Self is in control of your thought processes is that negative feelings are dominating. The two most common feeling categories experienced in a negative Primitive-Self are anger and fear. Anger, when present, is characterized by excessive blaming. You either blame others or yourself excessively. When fear is present, the individual is totally occupied with finding relief from it. Solutions to the experience of fear vary and include cognitive or overt behavioral obsessing, cutting off from all feeling, practicing any available addictive behavior, or finding a distracting activity that takes the individual's mind off the fear. These are all destructive, primitive options. Allowing them to occur reinforces the power of the Primitive-Self.

The solution to excessive emotions is to allow or demand the Meta-Self to take over control of thinking and address the negative experience. Intervention begins with allowing yourself to feel the emotion but require logical reasons for its occurrence. If you can identify no rational reason, then deny the experience of the feeling. It is considered irrational and is therefore discounted as being invalid. If the Meta-Self identifies a valid reason, then it searches for further understanding of the problem and creates a constructive solution.

A basic meta-principle for healthful living is to identify what you are afraid of and design a way to challenge it. Do not accept fear as a motivating or controlling force in your life. Choose courage—the courage to feel, and to examine the feeling and its cause for rationality and validity.

Take, for example, Jake's unexplained episode of anxiety and fear:

> I left here the other day feeling really good about myself. I felt light—a focused buzz. I felt light, like a great weight had been lifted. I was not sure what it was. It felt good. It lasted for about four days and then vanished. Then I started getting this pressure on my chest. I don't understand what it means. I talked to Ben at work about my experience, and I was trying to describe how I felt—what had happened in me. I just don't know what the feeling of pressure was. Since the good feeling left, I've had this heavy pressure in my chest that just won't go away.

Jake was feeling happy and exposed himself as being happy ("light") to his friend. His friend confirmed his good feeling just by listening. Jake's Primitive-Self reacted to Jake being happy by generating fear. "I'm not supposed to be happy. Something terrible is going to happen. It's not like me to be happy." Jake was overcome with a fear that something bad would happen, and he was out of his comfort zone of being cautious, unhappy, and afraid. Jake actually experienced being happy for four days and was not completely aware what it was—nor did he trust it. Since then, he has been feeling fear that will not go away. His Primitive-Self is fighting to reassert its power. Jake must learn to be happy. He must reassure his Primitive-Self and overrule its attempts to take back power from his Meta-Self. It will take time and many failed attempts for Jake to learn to live in his Meta-Self and trust being a happy person.

Building Your Meta-Self Through Interpersonal Skills Development

The Meta-Self must be lived to be learned. Remember the muscle-building analogy. Muscles must be used to grow. Mental muscle is the same. The more you use your meta muscles, the faster they will grow, and the more power they will gain in directing your thought processes.

Hold yourself accountable for relating with others while in

your Meta-Self; it improves your ability to relate effectively with others, and it challenges you by putting you more in touch with your real self. Additionally, relating effectively with others nourishes relationships and allows you to be nourished.

Interpersonal skills are abilities and methods of human interaction that demonstrate the capability to communicate empathetically with yourself and others. Included in these skills are objective listening skills, discrimination skills, and empathetic communication skills. Becoming proficient in these skills opens communication, demonstrates understanding, and leads to closer, more fulfilling relationships.

Objective Listening Skills

How often do others really listen to you? How often are you really understood? If your experience is like that of most people, being listened to and understood is rare. Most people are much more interested in themselves and in what they think.

Think back to someone in your past that made you feel special or valued. Without exception, they are people who listened to you and valued your thoughts and feelings. They may not have agreed with you, but you felt heard and understood.

Objective listening begins with putting your thoughts, feelings, opinions, needs, and anything else that concerns you aside. Instead, you mentally commit to getting into the other person's head and listening to her frame of reference—her perception. Putting your own thoughts and feelings on a shelf is not easy at first, particularly if you have a lot of issues of your own and tend to be overly self-focused. Another way to say this is that if you are dominated by your Primitive-Self, you will have little energy or interpersonal ability to connect with or even know how to focus on another person's perception. Therefore, to be successful you must get into and relate from your Meta-Self to develop and effectively employ objective listening skills or any interpersonal skills.

Discrimination Skills

Discrimination capabilities are best described as the cognitive ability to read other people. People are always communicating information about what they are thinking, feeling, and doing. In fact, it is said that it is impossible for people to avoid communicating about themselves. An individual with good discrimination skills excels at reading what another person is really saying or meaning, often in spite of his spoken words. He knows that only about 7 percent of what a person is communicating is the actual words spoken. A skilled person observes body movement, eye contact, voice inflection, and even what is left unsaid or avoided.

Empathetic Communication Skills

Empathy is the ability to hear, comprehend, and *communicate* an accurate understanding of another's personal experience (feelings and reasons) in the moment, from the other person's frame of reference. The communication of empathetic understanding is an objective skill. It is not the same thing as sympathy. Sympathy requires only the passive internal sharing of another's feelings. Empathy is the objective, unemotional communication of your understanding of the other person's perception of his experience.

Interpersonal skills are learned human skills. We are born with the capacity to learn them, but they are not automatic. Interpersonal ability is developed in, and is the sole province of, one's Meta-Self. Your level of ability to learn and display competence in these skills is interdependent with the developmental level of your Meta-Self; therefore, practicing these skills is also a method of developing your Meta-Self, because you must be connected to your real self to employ them. The level of introspective (internal) empathy you have about you determines your level of empathic ability with others. Remember, you must have empathy for yourself before you can have empathy for others.

Building your Meta-Self—Program Development Skills

By this point in your self-change effort you have established some new goals for thinking and behaving differently, yet you are unsure about how to achieve them. Repeating the exercises I have presented has worked to get you started in the right direction, but you want to do more to ensure your success. The answer lies once again in developing new abilities in your Meta-Self. In this case, it is developing your reasoning, organizing, and planning abilities. You need to gain proficiency in conceiving and planning efficient programs that will focus your learning efforts and therefore increase the probability of getting to where you want to be.

In reading this book and exploring your strengths and weaknesses, you have been introduced to unfamiliar knowledge of a psychological nature. That in itself makes changing yourself more difficult. But you are also facing the challenge of seeing and understanding yourself more objectively, and this too may add to your difficulties. In the psychological domain, where change is most difficult, program development skills are especially helpful. Hopefully, by this point in your efforts to change, you are familiar enough with the concepts I have presented and have a working knowledge of your deficits and the goals you want to achieve. Gaining proficiency in developing systematic programs will help you increase the probability of achieving those goals.

Before successfully applying program development skills to your self-change effort, you will need to be able to identify specific areas where you are having difficulty in achieving real change. Below are a few examples, but you should review your own unique experience to identify areas relevant to you that need special attention:

> » Consciously connecting with my real self

> » Overcoming my resistance to change

> » Staying in my Meta-Self

> » Relating to others with my healthy self

» Learning about reasoning

» Identifying constructive principles

» Building courage

» Staying in my Meta-Self when emotionally stressed

» Establishing and keeping boundaries in relationships

You may find it too difficult to be sufficiently objective about yourself, and therefore you will be unable to successfully specify your deficits and establish workable goals. Do not get discouraged. Find someone who can help you with your personal exploration, problem identification, and program development. Remember, changing yourself is not an easy goal to achieve. Do not hesitate to ask for help if the need arises.

For those readers who believe they are sufficiently objective about themselves to specify deficits and goals effectively, program development skills are appropriate; however, an adequate intro-duction to program development skills is not part of this book. In order to learn the necessary skills, you must consult other sources. There are many different resources for learning these skills, and you will need to access them to gain proficiency in planning and imple-menting effective programs. The Internet is a good place to begin searching for different perspectives about these skills.

Your first few attempts to write and implement a program will probably be only partially successful. Don't get discouraged. Identify what you do not know or what you have omitted from your program that made you unable to achieve your goal com-pletely, and try it again. Expect the necessity to conduct additional research to refine your skills. Be patient with your efforts. Like any new skill, you must perform it many times to gain proficiency. (See Appendix B for suggested sources.)

In Summary

Building your faith in your Meta-Self's abilities will not happen just because you have read this book and have had an intellectual insight that what I am saying makes sense to you. Your insight is important, but it is not enough. Psychological learning only occurs through intellectual insight *and* applied experience. You must use daily self-monitoring and structured practice to develop and live consistently in your Meta-Self. Don't forget you are good at fooling yourself, and therefore it is inevitable that you will slide back into Primitive-Self thinking. Building your ability to live in your healthy self will be a trial-and-error process for some time. You will make progress, and then you will catch yourself thinking or behaving in old, self-defeating ways. Each time this occurs, it means that more growth is possible. There is more to learn, more to make conscious, at deeper levels of your self.

Each time you falter, go back to the beginning of the discovery process. Start with centering on your feelings. Let go and actually feel, to identify a specific feeling or feelings. Look for new reasons about yourself that underlie each feeling. Your goal is to learn something new about your real inner self. Remember to stay out of your head. Do not rely solely on intellectual thinking to give you new information. It is imperative to couple feeling and thinking to discover deeper levels of your self.

Once you have discovered a new level of your Primitive-Self thinking, congratulate yourself, then get to work. Switch your thinking to your Meta-Self, and evaluate the validity of your self-discovery. Conclude your learning by responding to your Primitive-Self with the perspective of your healthy Meta-Self. Always end your thinking sessions with constructive Meta-Self responses, perspectives, and solutions.

As you achieve success in learning how to govern your life from the perspective of your Meta-Self, be sure to document in writing your new beliefs and principles. Building your conscious set of meta-principles will take time because you will need to have sufficient experience and learn by trial and error. As you identify and form your principles, remember that they must be constructive, logical, and congruent. With time and consistent effort you will experience an improved and stable perception of yourself and a belief in your ability to make sense of anything and solve it. You will gain trust in your ability to identify truth and live it. As you refine your Meta-Self's content and processes, you will acquire enduring faith in your ability to effectively guide your continued growth and fulfillment as a healthy individual.

Afterword

Psychologically healthy people and those who want to be psychologically healthy are motivated by courage—the courage to know the truth about their real selves and challenge anything they discover that impedes their health and fulfillment as human beings. They have courage as a primary motivator because they have faith in themselves and faith in their abilities. They have courage because they trust their own minds to know truth and guide them to attempt anything that will make their lives richer and more rewarding. They consistently challenge adversity and grow as human beings from the experience. They experience a life of valuing and respecting themselves. They are also adept at fulfilling their own needs and desires while respecting the rights and needs of others. They have the ability to live a life of psychological quality.

The concepts presented in this book have helped many people to improve the psychological quality of their lives. I hope that, for you, my book has been as eye-opening and motivating as it was intended. At the very least you should have gained some insight as to the real cause of many psychological problems, and perhaps your own.

Those of you who have attempted self-change have surely discovered that changing yourself for the better is not an easy task. A primary reason for this is that it is challenging to be objective about yourself. It is also difficult to hold yourself accountable for consistently thinking and behaving responsibly. It is much easier to see how other people behave irresponsibly, contradict what they say they believe, and harm themselves and those they care about.

By the way, you may try to share what you have learned in this book with others whom you believe could benefit from its message. Remember, regardless of how much you know they need help, you can only help those who own that they have problems and truly want help to change. It is always best to wait until someone asks for help. Finally, don't take it personally if they do not follow your advice. People have to be at the point in their lives where they are ready to commit to and pursue real change.

I hope that by this time in your efforts to change, you are beginning to experience yourself more positively and are well on your way to becoming who you want to be. After you experience some improvement, it may be tempting to rest on your laurels, to stop focusing on the growth process. After all that you have been through, a little bit of improvement can feel really good. Soon, however, you may find yourself regressing to old, primitive beliefs and behaviors. This is a clear indication that you have much more work to do. And remember, you were behind in self-development when you started the process of change, so you have a lot of catching up before you reach where you should be at your age. Don't be hard on yourself when you catch yourself regressing; just get back to work on developing your Meta-Self. Remember meta-principle number three: your efforts to grow as a person should never stop. Personal growth must be a lifelong pursuit, an integral part of your everyday experience. It is my firm belief that when you stop learning and growing as a person, you begin dying.

As you attempt to apply the philosophy and change process introduced in my book, you may find that you can only go so far in your self-help effort. Do not get discouraged; changing who you are at the deepest level is perhaps the most difficult task anyone can undertake. You may not be able to complete your change process on your own. You may need to find a competent professional helper.

Looking for a competent mental-health professional may at first appear to be an easy task. The phone book is full of degreed and nondegreed people who practice the helping arts. Your problem will be to actually find a helper who is both mentally healthy and clinically competent at a high level. By mentally healthy I mean that the person you seek help from must be healthier than you. He or she must have already achieved the level of self-development that you seek. A helper cannot lead you to a place they have not been. By clinically competent I mean that he or she must be able to understand the concepts of self-psychology and be able to provide new knowledge and direction at the highest level.

Following are a few guidelines for you to use to evaluate a perspective helper. You must trust your own judgment to pick a competent helper. Choosing a helper is much like dating. Sometimes you know right away that a person is wrong for you. Others you have to see a few times, to get through the dating behavior and see the real person. In choosing your helper you may have to invest in several visits to complete your evaluation. Here are a few guidelines for assessing a prospective helper:

Do they treat you with respect and caring, or do they act superior and remain aloof and disconnected?

Do they respond with impatience or annoyance to your questions, or do they respond with patience and answers that you can understand?

Do they provide direction in identifying and solving your problem, or do they just listen and repeatedly tell you how you feel?

Do you have a sense that the helper understands you and your problem?

Do they verbally communicate this understanding to you in a way you can understand?

Do they communicate understandable and logical goals for your treatment?

Remember, it is your responsibility to choose wisely. Pick a helper who fits the bill. Don't accept anyone as a helper just because they have a degree or certification. Use the above principles as a beginning guide. Above all, choose someone who knows more than you do and makes you work hard to learn, and choose someone you cannot fool. If you can fool your helper, you will get no help. You are only fooling yourself and allowing your Primitive-Self to remain in control.

In Closing

The capacity to change one's self for the better is in each of us. It is up to you to decide to change the course and quality of your life. You must take conscious responsibility for who you are and for becoming who you want to be. You must choose to learn to like and love yourself, and you must pursue this goal until it is your reality. Regardless of previous history, it is within your power to constructively shape the processes of your own mind and the direction and quality of your future. To accomplish this task, you must develop your Meta-Self—your responsible, healthy, mature self. There is no other path to experiencing true and enduring psychological quality.

The development of your Meta-Self begins with adopting and living the three universal meta-principles that are fundamental to all other beneficial psychological principles and values.

Universal Meta-Self Principles

» To know, value, and live in functional reality—truth

» To know, value, and live conscious, constructive, reasoned thinking

» To know, value, and live a lifestyle of psychological growth

Major Meta-Self Principles

» Being consciously connected to all facets of your self and in constructive control of your thinking, feeling, and actions

» Being proactive in holding yourself accountable for initiating beneficial, constructive thinking and actions

» Being responsible and self-accountable for and to yourself—physically, intellectually, and psychologically

» Being focused on reality—identifying and accepting objective and functional truth, and living it

» Being empathetically connected to yourself and others, with focus on genuineness, respect, understanding, and constructive action

» Being committed to growth as a human being to the limit of your personal potential

As you master these principles and add your own to them, you will begin almost immediately to experience the fruits of your efforts. You will begin believing in and valuing you. You will be able to accept the nourishment of others, because you believe you are worthy, and you will be able to give nourishment to others. Only by consciously developing a healthy self, a Meta-Self, will you or anyone be able to experience true and consistent psychological quality—the essence of a life lived well.

C. Franklin Truan, PhD

—

Appendix A: Sample of Feeling Words

Abandoned	Absorbed	Accepting	Admiring
Adoring	Affectionate	Affirmative	Affronted
Afraid	Aggravated	Agitated	Alarmed
Amazed	Ambitious	Amorous	Angry
Annoyed	Anxious	Apathetic	Apprehensive
Ashamed	Attracted	Awed	Besmirched
Bewildered	Bitter	Bleak	Blissful
Bored	Bothered	Brave	Bright
Broken	Buoyant	Calm	Capricious
Captivated	Carefree	Caring	Cautious
Certain	Changeable	Cheerful	Cheerless
Close	Comfortable	Compassionate	Complacent
Concerned	Confident	Confused	Considerate
Contemptuous	Contented	Converted	Convinced
Corrupted	Courageous	Cross	Cruel
Crushed	Curious	Cynical	Damaged
Defeated	Defensive	Defiant	Defiled
Definite	Degraded	Delicate	Delighted
Depressed	Desecrated	Despairing	Desperate
Despoiled	Determined	Devoted	Dirtied
Disappointed	Disbelieving	Discouraged	Disgraced
Disheartened	Dishonored	Disillusioned	Dismal
Disobedient	Displeased	Disregarded	Distant

Appendix A: Sample of Feeling Words

Distraught	Distressed	Distrustful	Disturbed
Doubtful	Dreary	Dubious	Dull
Eager	Earnest	Ecstatic	Edgy
Elated	Embarrassed	Empowered	Enchanted
Encouraged	Engaged	Engrossed	Enraged
Enraptured	Enthralled	Enthusiastic	Erratic
Evasive	Exalted	Exasperated	Excited
Exhilarated	Exultant	Fantastic	Fascinated
Fearful	Festive	Fouled	Friendly
Frightened	Frustrated	Furious	Glad
Gloomy	Goaded	Grateful	Grieving
Grim	Gripped	Grumpy	Harmed
Hateful	Heartbroken	Heated	Held
Helpful	Helpless	Hesitant	Hopeful
Hopeless	Horrified	Hostile	Humble
Humiliated	Hurt	Hysterical	Ignored
Immersed	Impaired	Impatient	Impulsive
Incensed	Inconsistent	Indecisive	Independent
Indifferent	Indignant	Infuriated	Injured
Inquisitive	Insecure	Inspired	Intent
Interested	Intrigued	Involved	Irate
Irresolute	Irritated	Jealous	Joyful
Joyous	Jubilant	Jumpy	Kind
Light-hearted	Livid	Lonely	Loving
Low	Loyal	Mad	Marred
Mean	Melancholy	Mesmerized	Messed up
Miserable	Misunderstood	Moody	Mortified
Murky	Nervous	Obsessed	Offended
Ominous	Open	Optimistic	Outraged
Overwrought	Panicked	Passionate	Patient
Peaceful	Peeved	Persuaded	Perturbed
Pessimistic	Petrified	Pitying	Playful
Pleasant	Pleased	Poignant	Positive

Appendix A: Sample of Feeling Words

Powerless	Preoccupied	Proud	Provoked
Puzzled	Raging	Rancorous	Rapt
Raving	Regretful	Rejected	Relaxed
Relieved	Remorseful	Resentful	Respectful
Ruined	Sad	Sanguine	Satisfied
Scared	Skeptical	Secure	Seething
Serene	Shaky	Shamed	Shocked
Shy	Soiled	Somber	Sorrowful
Spellbound	Spiteful	Spoiled	Strained
Strong	Stubborn	Stupid	Sulky
Sullied	Sure	Suspicious	Sympathetic
Tainted	Tarnished	Tender	Tense
Terrified	Threatened	Thrilled	Timid
Torn	Tranquil	Triumphant	Troubled
Trusting	Ugly	Uncertain	Uncomfortable
Unconvinced	Understanding	Undetermined	Uneasy
Unforgiving	Uninformed	Uninviting	Unnerved
Unnoticed	Unpredictable	Unreliable	Unsure
Unwanted	Upbeat	Upset	Vacillating
Variable	Vengeful	Vexed	Violated
Volatile	Warm	Wavering	Weak
Worried	Wounded		

Appendix B: Suggested Reading

Reading to Promote Connection with Real Self

Honoring the Self, by Nathaniel Branden
The Art of Living Consciously, by Nathaniel Branden

Reading about Reasoned Thinking and Logic

Nonsense: A Handbook of Logical Fallacies, by Robert J. Gula
Objectivism: The Philosophy of Ayn Rand, edited by Leonard Peikoff

Additional Reading in Psychology

Meta-Values: Universal Principles for a Sane World, by C. Franklin Truan, PhD
On Becoming a Person, by Carl Rogers
The Art of Loving, by Erich Fromm
The Virtue of Selfishness, by Ayn Rand

Program Development Skills

The Art of Program Development, by Robert R. Carkhuff

About the Author
C. Franklin Truan, PhD

Dr. C. Franklin Truan is a clinical psychologist who has been a practitioner in the field of mental health for forty years. He has been in private practice as a psychologist for thirty years, taught at several universities, authored articles in clinical psychology and interpersonal relations, and consulted with numerous public- and private-sector organizations.

Dr. Truan maintains that the best solution to mental illness lies in preventive psychological and interpersonal education, and in constructive social change. On an individual level, healthy psychological development and the experience of psychological quality require a nurturing early-life environment and a lifelong commitment to acquiring new knowledge, understanding, and the pursuit of personal growth.

In his previous work, *Meta-Values: Universal Principles for a Sane World*, Dr. Truan used commonsense language to transform complicated concepts from the fields of philosophy and psychology into useful knowledge about the critical relationship between the values individuals and societies choose to live and their level of acquired mental health. In this work, Dr. Truan demonstrated the powerful relationship between our actual lived values and beliefs, and our ability to experience psychological quality as individuals or as a society. Dr. Truan further maintains that philosophy and psychology are the provinces of everyone and therefore practical knowledge from these disciplines is essential in improving the mental health and personal fulfillment of every individual. Additionally, he maintains that the meta-values as presented are universal in application and therefore fundamental to forming a rational and ethical value structure that will lead to peaceful, beneficial relationships among all people.

In this current work, *My Enemy, My Self: Overcoming Your Self-Defeating Mind*, Dr. Truan provides a self-help guide for constructive psychological self-change. Dr. Truan presents an easy-to-understand step-by-step process for developing a positive self-concept. Based on the contributions of others in the field of self psychology and on his own clinical experience, Dr. Truan uses simple language to explain difficult psychological concepts about the self, the causes of poor self-concept, and its relationship to the many psychological problems experienced by millions. In addition, he explores how an individual's mind can be a constructive ally to psychological self-development or a limiting or destructive enemy to an individual's development and fulfillment in life. Through the development of one's Meta-Self—the portion of the mind that knows truth, takes responsibility, and displays courage—any individual can significantly improve the psychological quality of his or her life.

To contact Dr. Truan, visit his website at CFTruan.com.

CPSIA information can be obtained at www.ICGtesting.com
Printed in the USA
DW12s2322211213
359LV00004B/516/P